The Conservative
Investor's Guide
to Trading Options

Other Wiley Investment Books

Cyber-Investing: Cracking Wall Street with Your PC, Second Edition
David L. Brown and Kassandra Bentley

The Investor's Anthology: Original Ideas from the Industry's Greatest Minds
Charles Ellis with James R. Vertin

Mutual Funds on the Net: Making Money Online
Paul B. Farrell

Independently Wealthy: How to Build Wealth in the New Economic Era
Robert Goodman

The Conservative Investor's Guide to Trading Options
LeRoy Gross

Merton Miller On Derivatives
Merton Miller

REITs: Building Your Profits with Real Estate Investment Trusts
John Mullaney

The Art of Short Selling
Kathryn F. Staley

The Stock Market, Seventh Edition
Richard J. Teweles and Edward S. Bradley

The Conservative Investor's Guide to Trading Options

LeRoy Gross

John Wiley & Sons, Inc.

New York • Chichester • Weinheim • Brisbane • Singapore • Toronto

Published by John Wiley & Sons, Inc.
Published simultaneously in Canada.

This publication is designed to provide accurate and authoritative information in regard to the subject matter covered. It is sold with the understanding that the publisher is not engaged in rendering professional services. If professional advice or other expert assistance is required, the services of a competent professional person should be sought.

Library of Congress Cataloging-in-Publication Data:

Gross, LeRoy.
    The conservative investor's guide to trading options / LeRoy
Gross.
        p.   cm.
    Includes Index.
    ISBN 0-471-31585-0 (cloth : alk. paper)
    1. Stock options. I. Title.
HG6042.G76 1999   98-24239
332.63′228—dc21

This book is dedicated to:

My grandchildren:
  Malka Chaya Rabinowitz
  Chava Tova Rabinowitz
  Kiel Arin Gross
  Marcus Everette Gross
  Tyler Ari Gross

Their parents:
  Linda and Irvin Rabinowitz
  Cindy and Terence Gross

My other children and spouse:
  Daniel Gross
  Paula and Ralph Camilli

My wife:
  Leah June Gross
  who served unfailingly and lovingly as
  my own personal critic, secretary, moti-
  vator, lover, best friend.

  With my love to you all for the great
  happiness each of you brought to me.

Foreword

Derivatives have become an important tool for an ever-increasing number of investors. The broad definition of *derivatives* includes options, futures, and many more exotic instruments that are conjured up by the leading investment banks. For most stock-oriented investors, though, the term predominantly refers to stock options. The virtual explosion in trading of stock options attests to their importance.

Still, there are many who do not yet understand what stock options are or how they can be of benefit to an investor. This book is for those investors. While it doesn't specifically address futures or index options, the groundwork that it lays will make it easy for the reader to later acquire an understanding of those types of options as well.

In reality, "an option is an option"—a call option gives one the right to acquire something at a specified price, and the option is only good for a predetermined period of time. That statement is true whether one is discussing an option to buy a piece of real estate, a stock, a futures contract, or any other more complicated entity. Thus, the basic information available herein should stand one in good stead, no matter what type of option one eventually trades.

This book begins with the simple concept of how to find, read, and understand stock option quotes in the newspaper. Then it explains the procedures required for order entry and has some treatment of commissions before beginning the discussion of strategies.

The remainder of the first half of the book is devoted to the strategies that most novice option traders employ: covered call writing, put buying—mainly for protection of stocks that are in one's portfolio—put selling as a means of eventually buying stocks at low cost, and some offshoots from these strategies. You may have noticed that option *buying* is not on the preceding list—for the author feels that this is a strategy that is not for the conservative investor.

I'd estimate that 75% of individual stock option traders—those who are trading for their own accounts—use only the strategies described in the first half of this book, once they've advanced past the stage of merely buying options for speculation. This is not to say that one shouldn't learn about strategies and perhaps utilize them, but just to point out that many investors don't feel the need to get too "fancy"—they are quite happy with the simpler strategies.

In the second half of the book, more sophisticated strategies are examined—but the author takes the bent that they are not for the conservative investor. These include naked writing and certain types of option spread strategies.

I knew LeRoy Gross before I ever came to Wall Street, and I think just about everyone involved in options did, too—from the old put and call dealers to the traders and managers in most of the brokerage firms' option departments.

I can still remember LeRoy saying, "Calendar spreads aren't worth the trouble. You have to be right twice to make any money, and that's just too much to ask for." What he meant was that you had to hope for the short option in the spread to expire worthless, and *then* you had to hope for the stock to move favorably to make your long option worth something consequential. In this book, LeRoy isn't quite so dogmatic, but the calendar spread is still among those "strategies conservative investors should avoid."

This is an example of what LeRoy means by his title of option trading for the *conservative* investor. And that is what I like about this book—it has plenty of tips on how to stay out of trouble. For most novice investors, avoiding the pitfalls is far more important than making big profits. Big profits will come if big losses haven't preceded them and wiped out one's capital.

This is not to say that the author gives a biased treatment of the more advanced types of strategies, such as spreads or naked writing. While their discussion falls under his general heading of strategies that are not for the conservative investor, he does not denigrate them. Rather, he treats them in a rational manner but takes care to point out that they may require more work, entail more risk, and generally necessitate more of a trader's mentality than the average conservative investor needs or wants to employ.

LeRoy Gross—at least in my opinion—was noted for three things in his business career: his knowledge of options, his sense of humor, and his superb ability as a salesman. This book is a distillation of LeRoy's vast knowledge of options, and unfortunately this book does not contain any of his humor. Much of it was business-related. He used to explain the CBOE's market maker system with a series of jokes that left attendees at his seminars rolling in the aisles.

His ability as a salesman is probably best related by the following story, although I'm sure that many others who knew him could relate similar tales. Back in about 1975—when the listed option market was about two years old (the CBOE began trading listed options in April 1973)—I was already publishing an independent weekly stock options newsletter, called *Hedged Option Strategies*. It was fairly sophisticated and entailed strategies such as ratio writes, ratio spreads, and others. I bumped into LeRoy somewhere, and he told me that he was giving a Saturday seminar at their New York Office (he was with Reynolds Securities). Now here I was writing one of the most advanced option letters of the day, and LeRoy was trying to talk me into going to his rather introductory option seminar. Did I attend? Of course I did. No one could resist LeRoy's sales approach.

This book isn't really a sales piece for options—although I'm sure LeRoy could have done a great job on such a book. But, then again, maybe in a certain sense it *is*—for the more knowledgeable that the public is about trading options, the more they will benefit. I, of course, am a firm believer in the usefulness of options to nearly all investors—conservative or aggressive—for they can be tailored to any approach one might want to take to investing.

This book therefore makes a good starting point for the stock trader who wants to get involved with options, and it should prove to be a good springboard into further knowledge of the subject.

LAWRENCE G. MCMILLAN

Preface

Many books have been written about the listed option market, and I have no doubt that many more will be published after this one. Many of the existing books are replete with complicated graphs and mathematical curves that are more easily understood by individuals who have extensive knowledge of algebra and higher mathematics. Those readers without a distinct mathematical bent have difficulty in readily comprehending the various strategies and their consequences.

Furthermore many of the existing option books extensively use the jargon of the option world—words and phrases that are difficult to absorb and understand except by the deeply initiated.

In this book I have tried to make clearly understandable, even to neophytes, the various option strategies most frequently employed with individual stocks. Wherever possible, I have purposely tried to avoid the language of the option world, such as the following:

- Exercise.
- Straddle.
- Combination.
- Assignment.
- Spread.
- Strike price.
- Put.
- Roll-up.
- Roll-out.
- Call.
- Roll-down.

These terms and others are defined in the Glossary at the end of the book.

By using "people" language throughout the book, I hope that you will be able to readily comprehend and put to use in your own portfolios the more basic and conservative option strategies.

I have also made a great effort to carefully point out the various risks and degrees of risk that accompany each strategy. A risk-informed investor is usually a better investor. Careful reading and rereading of the various chapters dealing with strategy should help an investor be better able to (1) increase stock income, (2) reduce stock risk, and (3) seek stock profits.

The perceptive reader will also note that there is very little material and information regarding the tax consequences of the various strategies. The omission is deliberate because of our rapidly changing tax laws. Each year seems to bring tax law changes that tend to diminish, change, or make obsolete certain option strategies.

The individual option investor should make every effort to keep up with and to understand the tax consequences of any option strategy by obtaining information from the IRS and from a CPA familiar with the tax consequences of dealing in options. Although this may be a difficult and burdensome chore, it is not impossible. Relying on your individual account executive for tax advice is not normally the best route to follow, although some account executives are well informed and up-to-date on the latest tax rulings regarding option transactions. Many are not, however, and brokerage firms that handle option accounts advise their clients to seek their own tax advisor *before* entering into option transactions. Most investors find that that advice is very difficult to carry out. It is particularly difficult if you are just testing the option market in a small way. Finding tax advisors who are knowledgeable about options can be an onerous job. The expense of getting the advice frequently is prohibitive for those investors willing to learn and accept some degree of risk.

WARNING

Option transactions are by their very nature complex. Many purveyors of option strategies attempt to oversimplify and to make readily understandable the various investment techniques that use options. The reality is that all option strategies have such a variety of complexities involving price, risk, time, and profit potential that a quick and easy grasp is not easily come by.

Before entering into any option strategy, you should assess yourself. If you are contemplating the execution of an option strategy and if you feel that you:

1. *Are uninformed,*
2. *Are poorly informed,*
3. *Are a careless recordkeeper,* or
4. *Do not like the pressure* of decision-making, *then don't execute the strategy.*

Despite all the problems and oft-quoted risks in executing option transactions, I believe that there are enough benefits available to make option strategy a helpful tool for most investors.

Acknowledgments

I would like to express my deep appreciation to some *very special people* who spent considerable time and effort in reading the manuscript and in offering many helpful suggestions to improve the readability:

Julian Friede is a long-time friend and retired investment executive who had a very successful brokerage career. His stock analytical ability and thorough knowledge of the option market made his opinions highly valued by his many clients and by me.

Dennis Newman is currently a senior vice president with Dean Witter Reynolds in Fort Lauderdale, Florida, and one of the most knowledgeable and ethical brokers in the securities industry. A member of the highly distinguished Chairman's Club, Dennis's input was most helpful.

Bay Gruber, along with his brother Renn, form one of the securities industry's "most successful partnerships." Bay formerly directed the broker training program for Dean Witter Reynolds, before deciding to join forces with brother Renn in Cape Coral, Florida. Their deep knowledge of the full range of investment products has made them almost invaluable to their clients and to their firm. The suggestions made for this manuscript were most beneficial.

Fred Dahl, a long-time member of the publishing industry, aided me through the laborious process of transforming "idea" into manuscript, into final print form. His expert grasp of all details from type size to book size and jacket design has contributed greatly not only to this book, but to my other books and to my videotapes.

To all of you go my heartfelt thanks, good wishes for your futures, and a copy for your personal library.

Contents

PART ONE

Option Strategies for Conservative Investors

CHAPTER 1

Reading and Understanding Option Tables

Before you enter into any listed stock option strategy, your prudent course is to take the time and the trouble to learn how to read and to interpret the option information published in various periodicals.

Gaining a clear understanding of the printed option results is not as simple a task as one would imagine. These periodicals often do one or more of the following:

- Use different abbreviations to identify the stock underlying the option contracts.
- Supply statistical data that are unexplained.
- Omit certain statistical data as a space-saving device.

The primary sources that identify listed option trading results are the following:

- Daily papers of large cities.
- The *Wall Street Journal*.
- *Barron's Weekly*.

Most daily papers outside of Los Angeles, New York, and Chicago often omit option trading results on exchanges other than the Chicago Board Options Exchange (CBOE) and the American Stock Exchange (AMEX). This deficiency plus other problems, such as a small type size, make local papers a secondary source of information on option results.

For most investors the easy availability of the *Wall Street Journal* makes it the paper of choice for daily option results because of its large readable type size and its coverage of option results on all option exchanges. *Barron's*, which comes out once each week, is also a very helpful tool for the option investor. In its compilation of option results, it supplies information not readily available elsewhere.

THE *WALL STREET JOURNAL*

Let's look carefully at the typical option information supplied in the *Wall Street Journal* and learn exactly what we mean by "information not readily available elsewhere."

The circled numerals in Table 1.1 refer to the following explanations of the various items in the table.

1. The *option close* is the final options closing price on the options exchange.

A *sales unit* is usually 100 shares, which means that each option contract is normally for 100 shares of the underlying common stock. Option contracts, however, are subject to adjustment to reflect stock splits, stock distributions, and stock dividends. Before you enter into any option strategy, be wary and ascertain the exact share number represented by the option contract in which you have an interest.

2. *ALCOA* is the name of the company whose shares underlie the option contract. Many times the ticker symbol is used—the company name is abbreviated, or letters are used to identify the company on the listing exchange that bear little or no resemblance to the actual company name.

Table 1.1   Listed Options Quotations, Wednesday, November 4, 19XX: Chicago Board

NYSE Close① Option: ALCOA②	Strike Price③	Calls (Last)⑤			Puts (Last)⑥		
		NOV	DEC	JAN④	NOV	DEC	JAN④
$41^1/_2$④	35	r⑧	r	r	$1^3/_{16}$	r	$1^7/_8$
$41^1/_2$	40	r	$4^1/_2$	r	$1^1/_2$	$2^7/_8$	r
$41^1/_2$	45	$3/_4$	$2$⑦	$2^3/_4$	r	r	r
$41^1/_2$	50	r	r	$1^1/_2$	r	r	$10^1/_2$
$41^1/_2$	55	r	r	$1/_2$	r	r	r
$41^1/_2$	60	$1/_{16}$	r	r	r	r	r
$41^1/_2$	65	r	s⑨	$1/_4$	s	s	r

If you don't know the ticker symbol for sure, ask before you enter an order. There are many lookalike and soundalike names. Why take the risk of some financial hurt by not inquiring before making a commitment?

3. The price of 41¹/2 is the closing price per share of the stock underlying the option contract for the date listed under the "Listed Option Quotations" column of the *Journal*.

4. The *strike price* is the price specified in the option contract and is expressed in dollars per share. As the stock price moves up or down, new strike prices are created in an effort to have some strike prices near the current stock price. The largest volume of option activity normally centers around (up or down) the strike price(s) nearest to the current market price.

As can be seen in Table 1.1, several different strike prices may be available for option investors to buy or write, each with its own degree of risk or potential reward. When you see many strike prices listed for a certain stock, you know that the stock has been extremely volatile in the recent past. It is a warning flag to investigate carefully before making a commitment to the stock or the option.

5. The columns of Table 1.1 that are headed "*Calls (Last)*" inform the investor that prices listed under the heading are for *call option contracts only*. Each call option contract normally represents the right for a purchaser to "call" for (to buy) 100 shares of the named stock at the strike price that is stated. Each contract is always subject to adjustment to reflect stock dividends, splits, and stock distributions.

The word *last* refers to the fact that the price shown is the last price at which the option traded on the date specified. The last price is often confusing to both brokers and investors. *The last trade on an option quite frequently occurs hours before the close of trading.* The *stock* price may have moved substantially up or down since the last trade on the option.

Investors perusing the *Journal* for bargains often are led astray by the last price quotation. When they attempt to get an option execution at or close to the last price, they are often dismayed or disappointed by the disparity between the last price and the current bids and offers. Gaining a proper understanding of available option information is certainly a good first step toward successful use of the listed option market.

6. The "*Puts (Last)*" heading tells the investor that the prices listed under it are for put option contracts only. Each put option contract normally represents the right of the put owner to sell 100 shares of the named stock at the price specified in the put contract. This right can be exercised at any time during the life of the put.

Put issuers obligate themselves to buy 100 shares (subject to adjustments as per terms of the contract) of the named stock at the price specified any time during the put life.

Learning how to interpret published option data is a giant step toward learning how to benefit through option use.

7. You will notice that under the heading "Calls (Last)" there are three expiration months listed for the call option contracts. Under each monthly heading are listed either numerals or letters.

The numerals stand for dollars per share for each share underlying the contract. (Remember that *most* contracts are for 100 shares of the underlying stock.) The price "2" means that $200 ($2 × 100) was paid by the call option buyer for the right to buy (call for) 100 shares of ALCOA stock at the strike price of $45 per share. That right would extend through only the December expiration period.

To be sure you are reading option result information correctly, place a ruler or straight edge just under the strike price and the option price. Then look at the vertical column under the expiration month heading in which you have an interest. In Table 1.1, you should note also the date of the option quotation, which was November 4, 19XX.

The call option buyer paying 2 ($2 × 100) would be obtaining the right to purchase 100 shares of ALCOA common stock (remember, subject to adjustments) at the $45 per share price from November 4 to the expiration date of the option in December of the same year.

That brings up another point that requires clarification. Many uninformed investors, in looking at option results published in the various papers and even in examining their own brokerage statements, have a belief that options owned or obligated for can be exercised or closed out any time before the end of the month. This is simply not true! All stock option contracts are due to expire (if not closed out or exercised) on the Saturday following the third Friday in the expiration month. If the first day of the month was a Friday, then the sixteenth day would be the date of expiration. If the seventh day of the month was a Friday, then the twenty-second day would be the date of expiration. Confused? You are not alone. Many brokers and others in the securities industry really do not know all the details, nuances, and complexities of the option market.

Another confusing point is that even though the right to exercise an option does not expire until the Saturday after the third Friday, option owners desiring to exercise their rights must do so by the Friday or the last business day preceding the Saturday expiration.

8. As you become more familiar with scanning the option results and trying to uncover opportunities, you will inevitably encounter letters listed where option prices are normally placed. The lowercase letter "r" simply means that there was an option available for trading at that particular strike price and for that particular expiration month. Despite the availability of the option, there were no reported trades made for

that day in that particular expiration month and at that particular specified strike price.

9. The lowercase letter "s" means that there was no option available to buy or sell at that particular strike price and for that particular expiration month. Even if an investor had desired to execute an order for an option marked with an "s," it simply could not have been done.

10. Listed stock options are normally traded in three cycles in order to distribute option activity more evenly.

One cycle calls for options to expire January, April, July, and October. A second cycle has options that expire February, May, August, and November. A third cycle has options that expire March, June, September, and December.

Normally, three of the four expiration months for each cycle are open for trading. That certainly sounds easy enough to understand. When one of the four months in the cycle expires, another expiration month is added. However, to create still more option interest and volume, it was decided by the exchanges to begin a pilot program of sequential expiration months as indicated in Table 1.2. However, the *Wall Street Journal* and local papers show option results for only three expiration months, even though others are available for trading and trading in those other contracts might be very active and beneficial for investors.

As you can see in Table 1.1, there are three expiration months shown for both puts and calls. All the expiration months are near-term months. There could be excellent option opportunities in the months not shown, *but to take advantage of them you must know what is not shown.* You can inquire through a brokerage firm as to what expiration months, strike prices, and option prices are available.

Table 1.2 Sequential Equity Expiration Months

January	FEB	MAR	APR	JULY
February	MAR	APR	JULY	OCT
March	APR	MAY	JULY	OCT
April	MAY	JUNE	JULY	OCT
May	JUNE	JULY	OCT	JAN
June	JULY	AUG	OCT	JAN
July	AUG	SEPT	OCT	JAN
August	SEPT	OCT	JAN	APR
September	OCT	NOV	JAN	APR
October	NOV	DEC	JAN	APR
November	DEC	JAN	APR	JULY
December	JAN	FEB	APR	JULY

Okay, by now you should feel fairly comfortable about your ability to read and comprehend the listed option quotation results as published in the *Wall Street Journal*. What additional option information could be helpful to you that is not contained in daily local papers of the *Wall Street Journal*? Primarily because of space and cost constraints, the local daily papers and the *Journal* do not print certain information about option results that could be very helpful:

- High and low prices for the option that day.
- The total volume of option contracts executed for a particular strike price and expiration month.

If you want to know the high and low prices as well as the volume for a particular option, simply contact a brokerage firm representative, who will have ready access to that information through a desktop computer terminal.

WARNING

To get that information from the broker, you must make contact after the market closes and while a representative is still there who can access the computer. The next day, that information will be "wiped" from the terminal memory.

BARRON'S WEEKLY

Barron's Weekly is a highly regarded investment publication, and it is usually available in most areas of the country on Saturday or Sunday. *Barron's* offers the investor who is interested in options a more comprehensive view of option trading than any other readily available publication. Its only drawback is that the information is weekly rather than daily.

Let's examine a sample (Figure 1.1) of the printed options results from *Barron's* for *equity options* on the Chicago Board Options Exchange. *Barron's* actually uses eight column headings to provide weekly information on equity option results to the investor. The following discussion explains the headings and what they mean.

Company Exch. Close/Strike Price

This heading is *not* totally accurate. In the column under this heading are listed three pieces of information:

Company Exch Close	Strike Price			Sales Vol	Open Int	Opt Exch	Week's High	Week's Low	Last Price	Net Chg
EQUITY OPTIONS										
ADC Tel	Aug	30		2573	3948	PC	4 1/4	3 3/8	3 3/4	− 3/4
A M R	Aug	75		2947	3391	AM	3 3/8	1 1/4	1 9/16	− 1/16
AT&T	Jan	55		1461	4980	CB	9	7	8 3/8	+ 1/8
60 5/8	Aug	60		4785	10054	CB	2 5/8	1 1/8	1 3/4	− 1/8
60 5/8	Oct	60		1529	6472	CB	4 1/8	2 3/4	3 3/4	+ 3/8
60 5/8	Aug	65		1407	10407	CB	5/8	1/4	5/16	− 1/8
60 5/8	Oct	65		1404	8406	CB	1 15/16	1 1/16	1 1/2	...
AccuStff	Aug	25	p	2414	640	CB	4 5/8	5/8	2 1/2	...
23 5/8	Aug	25		1516	853	CB	3 3/4	5/8	15/16	...
23 5/8	Aug	30		3488	1370	CB	1 1/8	3/16	3/8	− 1 3/16
AdvFibCm	Aug	20	p	2068	5386	AM	1 5/8	13/16	7/8	− 1/2
19 15/16	Sep	20		1584	197	AM	3 5/8	2 1/4	3 1/8	− 2 1/4
19 15/16	Dec	30		2053	2098	AM	1 11/16	3/4	1 11/16	+ 3/16
A M D	Aug	17 1/2		2158	4632	PC	1 1/2	3/8	1	+ 7/16
17 1/4	Jan	20		1232	8159	PC	2 3/4	1 5/8	2 1/4	+ 9/16
AirbFr	Aug	30		1376	1486	XC	2 1/8	1/4	1/4	− 1 7/8
23 7/8	Sep	30		1297	1218	XC	1	3/8	7/16	...
Airtch	Aug	60		1557	6102	XC	4 5/8	7/8	1 7/16	− 1 11/16
58 13/16	Aug	65		1463	8007	XC	1 5/8	3/16	5/16	− 11/16
Altera	Aug	40		2038	7334	XC	2 3/8	3/4	1 1/8	− 1/16
Amazon	Aug	95	p	3159	9372	XC	4 1/2	1 7/8	3	− 1/8
110 7/8	Aug	100	p	3319	11672	XC	6 5/8	2 3/8	4 1/4	+ 1/8
110 7/8	Aug	105	p	1331	5060	XC	9 3/8	4 1/8	6 1/8	+ 1 1/4
110 7/8	Aug	110	p	2860	7064	XC	11 1/2	4 1/2	8 1/4	+ 1 3/8
110 7/8	Aug	115	p	1562	4460	XC	14 1/8	6 1/4	10 3/4	+ 1 7/8
110 7/8	Aug	120	p	2849	5100	XC	17 3/4	8 5/8	13 5/8	+ 2 3/4
110 7/8	Aug	120		2047	6620	XC	15 1/8	4 1/2	5 3/4	− 8
110 7/8	Aug	125		1684	4136	XC	12 7/8	3 1/4	4 1/4	− 8 1/4
110 7/8	Aug	130		2348	12064	XC	10 1/2	2 3/16	3	− 6 3/4
110 7/8	Aug	135		1903	11376	XC	8 3/8	1 5/16	1 13/16	− 5 9/16
110 7/8	Aug	140		1621	8792	XC	6 1/2	1 5/16	1 9/16	− 4 9/16
110 7/8	Aug	155		1946	11732	XC	3 1/2	1/2	1/2	− 2 5/8
AmOnline	Aug	45		1692	5133	XC	2 9/16	3/4	1 9/16	− 7/8
117	Oct	75	p	4947	21018	XC	2 1/16	1 3/16	1 3/16	+ 11/16
117	Aug	100	p	3182	11892	XC	5 1/8	1 13/16	2 5/16	− 11/16
117	Aug	100		1604	5553	XC	24	13	19 5/8	− 2 1/8
117	Aug	105	p	2887	7689	XC	7 1/2	2 11/16	3 1/2	− 1/2
117	Aug	105		2014	5889	XC	19 5/8	10	16 1/4	− 3/8
117	Aug	110	p	4458	9084	XC	9 7/8	4	5 1/2	− 1
117	Aug	110		5451	9543	XC	16	7 1/4	13	− 2 5/8
117	Sep	110		1549	2649	XC	19 1/4	10 1/2	16 1/4	− 1
117	Aug	115	p	3769	10395	XC	12	5 3/8	7 1/8	− 3/4
117	Aug	115		13917	25833	XC	12 1/2	5 3/8	9 7/8	− 2 3/4
117	Sep	115		1797	2646	XC	16	8 1/2	13 5/8	− 2 1/8
117	Aug	120	p	1256	6123	XC	15 1/4	7 1/2	10 1/2	+ 5/8
117	Aug	120		14315	19272	XC	10	3 7/8	7 5/8	− 2 1/2
117	Sep	120		1624	4356	XC	13 1/2	6 5/8	11 1/8	− 1 7/8
117	Aug	125		11603	22134	XC	7 3/4	2 3/4	5 3/4	− 1 3/4
117	Sep	125		3028	6885	XC	11 1/8	5 1/2	9	− 3/4
117	Aug	130		14929	28323	XC	6 1/8	2 1/8	4 1/2	− 1 3/4
117	Sep	130		1869	6762	XC	9 1/4	4 1/2	7 1/4	− 1 1/2
117	Aug	135		4361	14946	XC	4 5/8	1 1/2	3 1/8	− 1 1/2
117	Aug	140		7687	23160	XC	3 1/4	1 1/8	2 1/8	− 1 1/8
117	Jan	140		1181	5823	XC	13 1/2	8 1/2	12	− 1/4
117	Aug	150		2586	6951	XC	1 13/16	1/2	1	− 1 5/16
117	Oct	150		1878	4830	XC	5 7/8	2 3/4	5 1/8	+ 1/8
AmBankrs	Aug	60		3093	4545	XC	1 5/8	5/8	1 5/16	+ 7/16
AmExpr	Aug	110		1403	2066	XC	5 7/8	1 3/4	3 1/2	+ 7/8
APwrCv	Dec	25	p	1530	5067	CB	1 1/8	1 1/8	1 1/8	...
32 1/4	Dec	30		1597	5278	CB	4	2	4	+ 1 1/4
AmStrs	Aug	25		1606	2164	CB	1	1/2	5/8	− 1/4

Figure 1.1 *Barron's* Equity Options. (Reprinted with permission of *Barron's*. Copyright © 1998 by Dow Jones & Company, Inc. All rights reserved worldwide.)

1. The name of the underlying company in full or abbreviated form.
2. The expiration month of the option contract.
3. The strike price stated in that particular contract. (*Caution*: If the letter "p" does not follow the strike price, that tells you that the

traded contracts were *call options*. Put option contracts are indicated by the letter "p.")

Sales Vol.

This heading tells the investor the *total number of contracts* that were traded for the week at the stated strike price and for a particular expiration month.

Open Int.

The number in the *open interest* column tells you the number of outstanding options at that particular strike price and for that particular expiration month that have not been the subject of a closing transaction.

- A very high number usually indicates an active and highly liquid option contract.
- A low number usually indicates a lack of interest and activity in that contract.
- Disparities between bids and offers are normally *lower* in high open interest contracts and *wider* in low open interest contracts.

Week's High/Week's Low

Prices listed in these two columns reflect the week's highest and lowest prices for the option. The price is given in dollars per share for each share underlying the option contract (normally 100 shares). In the example shown in Figure 1.1, the first price listed under "High" is $3 1/2$ ($3.50), which is $350 for the contract (3.5 × 100). Commissions are added to purchases and subtracted from sales. The first price listed under "Low" is $2 1/8$, which means $212.50 per 100-share contract. This visible trading range helps the investor to observe the volatility and perhaps aids in a better assay of future price moves.

Last Price

The figures listed in this column provide the last price at which that particular option traded on the *last trading day* of the week. Again, the price is expressed in dollars per share for each share underlying the option contract (normally 100 shares). In Figure 1.1, the first price is $3 1/4 × 100$ (or $325 for the contract). Commissions are added to purchases and subtracted from sales.

Net Chg.

The number given under "Net Chg." tells you the net movement up or down for the option for the particular week. "Net chg." is the *net* change in price for the option from the *preceding* week. By examining the stock's net change from the preceding week and noting the option's net change, you can gain some idea of the option's movement versus that of the stock.

I hope that after you have carefully read this chapter, you will feel better prepared to read and comprehend option information available to you in your hometown. With this comprehension, you also should be able to benefit greatly from the various option strategies that are detailed throughout this book.

CHAPTER 2

What You Should Know about Entering Option Orders

Once you have investigated the possibilities available to *seek profits* and to *reduce* or *limit risk* through options, you must determine how to effect executions in the least harmful way.

Buying and selling option contracts appears to be a very simple matter, particularly so to the uninitiated, or inexperienced, investor. Reader, beware, it is not!

Careful reading of existing option literature furnished by the various option exchanges or perusing many of the popular books extolling the potentials available in the option market does little to inform you about how to go about placing option orders.

You place option orders with a representative of a brokerage firm. The order is then transmitted to the option trading exchange that handles the specified option. Whether the order gets executed immediately, at a later date, or not at all depends on the type of order you give to the broker.

Therefore, to effect execution of an order at a reasonable price differential (from the last available or quoted price), you should become familiar with the basic kinds of option orders that are allowed. Let's examine the most common option orders and when and how you might use them.

MARKET ORDERS

A *market order* is an instruction to buy or to sell (as the case may be) a stated number of option contracts at the best possible price whenever that order reaches the trading post. When you place a market order, you must have convinced yourself that you want an execution right away and that you are willing to pay the asked price in case of a buy order or to accept the bid price in case of a sell order.

If you give the market order for a large number of contracts, there may be a series of executions obtained at varying prices on the same market order. Let's look at the following example.

Example

Stock XYZ is at 33; XYZ Jan 35 calls are quoted 2 bid, $2^1/4$ asked. If you are enthusiastic about the possible upmove in XYZ before the January expiration, you give your broker a market order to buy 30 XYZ Jan calls. Frequently, the order may be executed as follows:

- Bought 10 XYZ Jan 35 calls at $2^1/4$.
- Bought 10 XYZ Jan 35 calls at $2^5/16$.
- Bought 10 XYZ Jan 35 calls at $2^3/8$.

If there happens to be a large offering at the $2^1/4$ quoted price, it is possible that all 30 contracts in the order will be executed at the $2^1/4$ asked price.

If the market order is to sell 30 XYZ Jan 35s, the order may be executed as follows:

- Sold 10 XYZ Jan 35s at 2.
- Sold 10 XYZ Jan 35s at $1^7/8$.
- Sold 10 XYZ Jan 35s at $1^3/4$.

WARNING

1. If the stock market is exhibiting great volatility, market order executions can produce price executions that vary widely from the price prevailing at the time the order is placed.
2. If the market itself is relatively quiet but the stock underlying the option contract is very volatile as a result of some specific news or expectation, *beware*! In such a case, an investor placing market orders can expect price executions that vary widely from the price prevailing at the time the order is placed.

When should you use market orders? You should enter market orders when you want to be certain to get out of an existing option position or when you want to be certain that you establish an option position.

In those rare instances when a market order to buy results in a price execution lower than the asked price at the time you placed the order, you have bought into a deteriorating situation. Conversely, when your market order to sell results in a price execution greater than the bid prevailing at the time of order entry, you quickly become aware that you have sold into an improving situation.

LIMIT ORDERS

Many option investors who have entered the option arena by entering market orders have often been disappointed with the executed price. This has been particularly true in fast-moving volatile markets. Investors placing option orders often use as a price guide the current bid and the asked prices for the option.

In volatile situations, a market order to buy an option may be executed at a price far higher than the asked price at the time of order entry. A market order to sell an option may be executed at a price far lower than the bid price prevailing at the time of the order entry.

To avoid those possible unpleasant execution prices, all option exchanges provide investors with the opportunity to enter orders other than market orders. The most popular kind of option order in addition to the market order is the *limit order*. There are several kinds of limit orders. Let's examine each kind and the ways each can be used.

Day Limit Orders

A *day limit order* is an instruction given to the broker to do the following:

- Buy at a price no higher than the price specified by the investor. Of course, a purchase price below the specified limit is always welcome.

- Sell at a price no lower than the limit specified by the investor. Naturally, a sale at a price higher than the specified limit is welcome and is beneficial to the investor.

By using day limit orders, the investor avoids all unpleasant surprises as to price.

As the name implies, day limit orders are good only for the particular business day on which they are placed. Day limit orders can also be canceled, or the price limit can be changed by the investor during the day. *The investor entering the order to cancel should be aware that part or all of the order might have been executed before the cancellation of the order.*

The user of the day limit order must also recognize and accept the fact that the order may not be executed wholly or in part because of the price limit specified. This is true even if the limit given is equal to the price asked in case of a buy order or to the price bid in case of a sell order.

Touched Limits. Investors entering day limit orders should understand and learn the meaning of *touched limits*. See the following example.

Example

Stock XYZ is at 35; XYZ Jan 35 calls are 2 bid, 2 1/4 asked. An investor obtaining the current quote of XYZ Jan 35s from a broker authorizes the entering of a day order to buy 10 Jan 35s at 2 1/4. The broker enters the order as instructed and informs the investor that 20 XYZ Jan 35s traded at 2 1/4 after the investor's order was entered. The investor may think the order was executed. Maybe so—maybe not!

If no report of execution is received at the end of the day, the investor can ask the broker to check with the option exchange as to whether none, part, or all of the order was executed at the limit price specified. Trades that occur at the investor's limit price after the order has been received on the option exchange trading floor are called *touched limits*.

If no execution was reported on a touched limit and a volume of contracts seems to have been traded at the touched limit, the investor can request a computer printout report of all contracts traded after the order was received.

Sometimes an error does occur, and the printout helps to locate the problem. Mistakes are quite rare, but they do happen. It can never hurt to challenge a report of "nothing done" on a touched limit order. Touched limit orders usually go unexecuted because of the number of orders ahead at the same limit price.

Penetrated Limits. A *penetrated limit* is an entirely different thing. Using the same example, let's assume that the newspaper listing on the day after the order was entered showed the last price for XYZ Jan 35s to be 2³/₁₆. Because the order was to buy at 2¹/₄ (or less), the investor has to be guaranteed that all of the order was completed at the limit or better! *This is always true unless the newspaper report was erroneous.*

Stop Limit Orders

Another order that is used often is the *stop limit order*. Let's examine how it works.

Example

You have bought 10 XYZ Jan 35 calls for 3. The total risk is 10 × 100 × 3, or $3,000 plus the commission costs to buy and later to sell. (There is no sell commission if options expire worthless.) In an attempt to protect against a total loss, you tell your broker to enter a sell stop limit order at 2. The order is to remain in effect until executed or canceled. This order is simply a contingency order. As long as the option price remains above 2, nothing happens to the order.

If a single option contract trades at the 2 price, however, the order is triggered and automatically becomes a limit order to sell at the limit price of 2. Sounds good, doesn't it? All nice and neat. Lose some of the speculative funds, but not all.

Just suppose that XYZ Jan 35 calls decline to 2 and that the decline triggers the stop limit order to sell at 2. Suppose also that the next and subsequent trades are 1⁷/₈, 1³/₄, 1¹/₂. *You still have the entire risk of the position!* The stop order was triggered by the decline to the 2 price and became a limit order to sell at 2. Because the options traded below 2 after the order became effective, no execution at 2 was possible!

I really believe sell stop limit orders should be avoided by investors, both for options and for stocks. The risk of still remaining in a declining and unwanted position is simply too great.

STOP ORDERS

A widely used order is the *stop order*. Using the same situation as in the preceding example, let's see how this order works to get an investor out of a position that is no longer wanted.

Example

XYZ Jan 35s have been purchased at 3. Not wanting to risk the 100% loss of the funds invested, you instruct your broker to put in a sell stop order for 10 XYZ Jan 35s at 2. So long as XYZ Jan 35s do not trade at 2, your position is intact with relatively unlimited profit potential. Should XYZ Jan 35s trade down to 2, the sell stop order at 2 is converted to a market order to sell at the next price(s) after 2. *This order assures that you will be out of the position.* The next price after 2 could be above 2, at 2, or below 2. At least you are out with some of your investment recovered—which is the purpose of the stop order.

Stop orders can be very effective tools for controlling the emotional aspects of option trading. They are, in my opinion, far superior in every way to stop limit orders. For the risk-taking investor who opens a short option position, buy stop orders can be left in to help lessen the large risk that accompanies a short option position.

GOOD-'TIL-CANCELLED ORDERS

Good-'til-canceled (GTC) orders are those that are good until they are canceled by the investor. An order can be left in for a week, a month, or until expiration of the particular option. One of the advantages of GTC orders is not having to reenter unexecuted orders day by day. Still another advantage is the retention of your order's place in line.

Example 1

Let's suppose XYZ Jan 35 calls are trading steadily at 3. The bid price is $2^7/8$; the asked price is $3^1/8$. An investor who wants to establish a position enters an order: Buy 30 XYZ Jan 35 calls at 3 GTC. The broker enters the order and is informed "3 last, 5 ahead." This means that the last trade of XYZ Jan 35 calls was at 3, and that there is an order ahead of this one to "buy 5 at 3."

Once those five orders have traded at 3, the investor is entitled to all subsequent options that trade at 3 until his or her own order is complete. A GTC order may be completed in a day, a week, or a month or maybe not at all. But at least the investor retains the place in line at the 3 price for the term of the GTC order.

Investors buying or welling stock option contracts should make an effort to understand how GTC orders are adjusted to reflect the following:

- Stock splits.
- Reverse stock splits.
- Stock dividends.
- Stock distributions.

A GTC order entered into a specialist's or a board broker's book before the expiration date (exdate) of the distribution is automatically adjusted as to:

- Exercise price.
- Number of shares or contracts.
- Prices on the limit orders.

Example 2

1. An investor places a GTC order to buy 5 XYZ Jan 30s at 4.
2. XYZ declares a 2-for-1 split while the order is in effect.
3. After the exdate for the split, the order is adjusted as follows: "Buy 10 XYZ Jan 15 calls at 2 GTC."

Notice that before the exdate for the split, an order for "5 XYZ Jan 30 calls at 4," if executed, would involve the expenditure of $2,000 (5 × 400) plus commissions.

After the exdate and the adjustment to reflect the 2-for-1 split, the order, if executed, would be for "10 XYZ Jan 15 calls at 2," or $2,000 plus commissions.

Covered call writers in the foregoing example would have to retain the additional shares in order to remain covered.

An investor who places a GTC order must bear the responsibility of remembering that the order has been given and must not enter a subsequent market order or limit order *without* canceling the GTC order. To do otherwise is to be subject to a possible monetary loss. Prices on limit orders are rounded to the nearest 1/8 when a price of over 3 results and are rounded to the nearest 1/16 when a price of under 3 results.

NOT-HELD ORDERS

Not-held orders are not used frequently. Nevertheless, they are worthwhile when placing orders for thinly traded options. Not-held orders are used when entering market orders for options when the trading volume is quite light or inactive. The *not-held market order* gives the exchange floor broker discretion about the *price* at which the order is executed and the *time* of the order execution.

Example

Suppose you wish to buy 10 XYZ Jan 35s and the last price is 3. The quote is "2³/4 bid, 3¹/4 asked." Very little interest has been shown in the issue. If you gave the order simply as "buy at the market," the execution might resemble the following:

- Bought one at $3^1/_4$.
- Bought three at $3^3/_8$.
- Bought three at $2^1/_2$.
- Bought three at $3^5/_8$.

By marking the order "not held," you allow the floor broker who is in the crowd to use his or her best judgment about what to pay and when to execute the order.

On lightly traded options, I highly recommend using market orders with the not-held instruction. Not forcing an immediate execution provides a benefit that seems to outweigh the occasional misjudgment of a floor broker.

ALL-OR-NONE ORDERS

A helpful instruction to accompany certain limit orders for 5, 10, or more contracts is to have the order marked "all-or-none."

Example

Let's assume that you are an option investor who is attracted to XYZ Jan 35 calls.

- The bid price is $2^3/_4$.
- The asked price is $3^1/_8$.
- The last price is 3.

If you enter an order to "buy 10 XYZ Jan 35 calls at 3," it is possible that just one contract might be available at the 3 price. If you purchase only that one contract, the commission cost will be exorbitantly high, particularly so with discount brokerage firms and other firms that charge a high minimum commission for each transaction.

If the limit order is a GTC order, it is possible to buy one contract a day for several days or even one contract a day until the entire order is complete. Of course, the order could go unexecuted or be canceled. The one-a-day execution would impose severe commission costs on you, thereby greatly diminishing your profit potential.

The *all-or-none instruction* on the limit order ensures that you get the entire order filled at the limit specified (or at a better price if available), or the order goes unexecuted.

The slight disadvantage of using all-or-none is that you might miss out on getting some small part of a limit order filled. In my view, the advantages of all-or-none orders outweigh the disadvantages.

Commissions can be negotiated, so it might be possible to negotiate a very reduced commission charge on partially filled limit orders. If you can do this, then you might not want to give the all-or-none instruction.

In addition to understanding the basic type of option orders to enter, as an informed investor you should be aware of the following:

- Lightly traded options usually have wide price disparities between the bid price and the asked price.
- Premiums tend to be higher for volatile stocks and for high price/ earnings ratio stocks.
- Exchanges with high volume in options, such as the American Stock Exchange and the Chicago Board Options Exchange, normally provide the investor with "thicker" markets.
- High open interest normally is an indicator of a "thick," or actively traded, market.

CHAPTER 3

Commission Discounts Increase Your Return on Investment

Many investors are attracted to the option market as a vehicle for potentially increasing their return on stock investments or as a way of speculating for profits. Their initial interest is usually aroused by one or more of the following:

- A solicitation from a broker.
- A newspaper or magazine article extolling the virtues or benefits to be derived from option activity.
- Word-of-mouth success stories told to them by friends or acquaintances.
- The option exchanges' advertisements and literature.

Most investors who are new to the option world execute their first option transactions through full-service brokerage firms. They seem to feel that the large, well-known firms are more likely to provide a pathway to success in option trading through the following services offered by those firms:

- Guidance by an account executive.
- Analysis by the option department.
- Expertise in the execution of option orders.
- Computer-calculated strategies available to individual investors.

Experienced option investors often grant their option business to the large brokerage firms for the same reasons as do the neophytes. Both the neophyte investor and the experienced investor at the large brokerage firms obviously pay commissions both on stock purchases and sales and on option purchases and sales. A key factor in investors' success or failure in garnering profits from their activities is often the commissions that they must incur in executing stock and option orders.

Since 1975 both stock and option commissions have been negotiable items between investors and the firms with which they do business. *Neophyte option investors, as a group, tend to pay the full list price for the execution of orders!* This is quite often true even if the orders are of large size. By paying commissions that are higher than necessary, investors necessarily lower their potential return.

I have talked with thousands of investors (and brokers) about transactions in which the brokerage charges to the investor were at no discount from the highest list price. When I questioned why no discount was given, investors' answers fell into the following major categories:

- I was too embarrassed to ask for a commission discount.
- I didn't know that I might possibly get a commission discount.
- I was afraid that my broker wouldn't be as helpful if I asked for a discount.
- I wanted to reward my broker for the advice and help that I was getting.
- It is beneath my dignity to ask for a discount.

All the foregoing reasons really do not have much validity in the hard, real world of investing. You owe it to yourself to make a legitimate attempt to enhance the investment return on the capital you place at risk.

Paying less in commission costs in no way harms the strategy employed. Common sense certainly indicates that a strong effort be made by stock and option investors to negotiate commission discounts from the high list price offered by the major brokerage firms. Most major brokerage firms permit their account executives great leeway in granting discounts. The discounts can range up to 25% without manager approval. You can get even larger discounts through the manager, depending on the size and frequency of your transactions.

If you make your own decisions independently and execute transactions in size, the discount broker is a viable and satisfactory alternative to the full-service brokerage firm. The savings available to you through discounts from the full-service brokerage firm's list price can be quite substantial—substantial enough in many cases to make a significant difference in the percentage of return on your investment, as well as a substantial increase in dollars earned or losses prevented.

There is a viable alternative for you if you actively trade options and stocks. That alternative is to divide the business between the discount broker and the full-service firm. Give the volume of business to the discount firm while still rewarding the full-service broker with some business in return for providing you with the special services that you want.

The facts of life are that the full-service firm would rather have *some* business than *no* business and that once the full-service firm is aware that the bulk of your business is being routed through a discount broker, it will often be able to provide a discount large enough to compete with the discount broker. The discount offered may be large enough to make you rechannel the bulk of your business through the full-service firm where you can get the best of both worlds:

- Low commissions.
- Advice (if needed and desired).
- Computer analysis.
- Research.

Let's look at some typical examples of option and stock transactions made through a discount firm and through a full-service firm.

Example 1

The order is: "Buy 10 XYZ Jan 30 calls at 3."

Commission costs:

Full-service firm list price	$142
Discount firm list price	− 62
Difference	$ 80

This is $80 that could be in your pocket rather than in that of the full-service brokerage firm. That $80 saving equals 2.7% of the $3,000 invested!

If you had negotiated a 50% discount from the full-service firm (because of the total volume of activity in your account or the potential for substantial activity), the actual dollar disadvantage on the trade would be only $9. For that difference the services provided by the full-service firm might be worth it.

Example 2

The order is: "Buy 500 XYZ at 31. Sell 5 XYZ Jan 35 calls at 2."

Stock commission costs:

Full-service firm list price	$293
Discount firm list price	−108
Difference	$185

Option commission costs:

Full-service firm list price	$75
Discount firm list price	−37
Difference	$38

In this example, you can readily see that if you executed the orders through a discount broker rather than through a full-service broker, you would save a grand total of $223—on a rather simple and common transaction named "buy-write" (buy the stock and immediately sell calls backed by the stock just purchased).

The moral so far in this chapter is to get full-service firms to grant significant discounts from their list prices or to use the services of discount brokers. Lest you think I totally favor the use of discount brokers over full-service firms, let me hasten to correct that opinion. Many of the large brokerage firms do have experienced, knowledgeable, hard-working account executives whose opinions and guidance are worth paying commissions above what discount brokers might charge, but they certainly are not worth full list price. Not every office of the major brokerage firms has that experienced, knowledgeable option broker. Before agreeing to pay higher than discount prices for stock and option executions, you should thoroughly investigate the broker designated to handle your orders. Some questions that you should ask your would-be account executive might include the following:

- How long have you been a registered representative? (My requirement would be *at least* five years.)
- How long have you specialized in *stock option* transactions? (My requirement would be *at least* three years. You surely don't want this person to be learning on your money.)
- How long have you been with this particular firm? (My minimum would be *at least* three years, unless there was a substantial tenure at another firm.)

If the salesperson had reasonable longevity at another firm but is new to the firm you are considering, you should ask the manager about the representative. Included in your questions to the manager should be one about security rules violations as a possible reason for the move. Brokers with lawsuit histories and compliance violations should be avoided.

You must also satisfy yourself that you and your potential broker are on the same wavelength. You must make sure that the broker:

- Understands your investment goals.
- Understands what risks you are willing to accept.
- Understands that *you* are the decision maker.
- Is to supply you with the firm's research, computer assistance, option analysis, and execution.
- Is to offer judgments and opinions with the understanding that they may or may not be accepted.
- Knows your complete financial situation.

If the full-service brokerage office with which you would like to do business does not have an account executive experienced in option trading to service your account, you might just as well use a discounter or try other full-service firms.

If you do not have a knowledgeable broker, you can substitute a study of the option strategies. These strategies are easily available in booklets published by the American Stock Exchange and Chicago Board Options Exchange. Read a couple of option books (including this one!). Start your option experiences in a small way until you feel you have garnered a good understanding of the option strategies that seem suitable for helping you to accomplish your goals. However, there is really no good substitute for the following:

- Making your own decisions.
- Observing the results of those decisions.
- Investing through various market cycles.

Full-service brokerage firms often charge lower commissions than do discount brokerage firms, particularly when option investors execute option orders for one or two option contracts priced under $1 per contract. Discount brokers' *minimum* commission charges preclude most investors from experimenting with one or two very low-priced option contracts. Look at the following examples.

Example 1

The order is: "Sell 1 XYZ Jan 15 call at $7/8$."

Discount firm minimum commission	$34
Full-service list price	–17
Difference	$17

Example 2

The order is: "Buy 2 XYZ Jan 20 calls at $3/4$."

Discount firm minimum commission	$34
Full-service list price	–27
Difference	$ 7

As you can see, the full-service firm's commission costs are substantially less than the discount firm's minimum charge.

Remember, it is your money that is being invested and placed at risk! You owe it to yourself to negotiate commission discounts from full-service brokerage firms or to use the services of discount brokerage firms.

You automatically increase your return on investment (ROI) by decreasing your commission charges. When dealing with a full-service brokerage firm, be sure that it furnishes you with a current commission table. Then when you are negotiating and are offered a discount, you will be able to calculate the percentage of discount yourself. In that way you will be able to determine whether you wish to continue doing business with that full-service firm, go to another full-service firm, or go to a discount firm.

You should also understand that discount firms offer discounts from either 1975 fixed prices or current representative prices! Full-service firms that offer discounts do so from a list price that is higher than the 1975 fixed price!

CHAPTER 4

The Buy Stock–Write Call Strategy

HOW TO WRITE CALLS FOR INCOME AND PROFIT

Many books, pamphlets, and articles have been written detailing (and often advocating) an investment procedure known as *covered call writing*. The bulk of the written material on covered call writing focuses on the issuance of call options that are backed, or covered, by the actual ownership of the underlying stock shares. In the majority of the writings, the virtues of the procedure are so slanted as to make a reader believe the following:

- That the strategy is conservative.
- That the strategy is simple.
- That the strategy greatly reduces stock ownership risk.

My view, dear reader, differs greatly from the foregoing truisms. As you thoroughly read and reread this chapter, as well as the others in this book, I hope that your eyes will be opened to the following:

- The degree of risks involved in covered call writing.
- The complexities involved in covered call writing.
- The various types of reward potential in covered call writing.

An investor contemplating entering the arcane world of stock-backed covered call writing is faced with a myriad of decisions, including the following:

- Should calls be sold on low-cost stock shares already owned?
- Should stock be bought and calls immediately written on the just-purchased shares (the buy-write strategy)?
- If stock is to be bought and calls written, which stocks are to be chosen?
- What length of time is normally best for writers of call options? One-month calls? Three-month calls? Six-month calls? Nine-month calls?
- Should calls be written with the strike price higher than the current market price of the stock?
- Should calls be written with the strike price approximating the current market price of the stock?
- Should calls be written with the strike price below the current price of the stock?

The preceding are just some of the questions you must resolve *before* entering into active covered call writing. *Simple, it isn't!*

Calls Backed by Optionable Stock

First, let us examine covered call writing for investors who already own optionable shares. If you already own optionable stock shares and want to try writing calls to augment the income (if any) being paid, you should have a very clear understanding of the following at the onset of the investment adventure:

- The commission costs of getting into the option position and, at some later date, out of it.
- Any tax consequence that might result from the sale of the owned stock and option.
- The limitation imposed on the profit potential in the stock through issuing the call option.
- The various decisions that might have to be made during the life of the call.
- The extra recordkeeping involved as a result of being a call writer.

Writing Calls on Shares You Already Own

If you are contemplating writing calls on already owned stock shares, you may have a cost basis in those shares that:

- Is lower than the current market price.
- Approximates the current market price.
- Is higher than the current market price.

Let's examine writing calls against the owned stock on the basis of the three different cost structures.

Cost Basis Lower than the Market. Stock XYZ is at 36. You originally bought shares at 26. In early January, you can write XYZ April* calls as follows:

Strike Price	Option Price
35	5
40	2¹/4
45	1

If you choose to accept the largest premium of 5 ($5 × 100 shares), you will be paid $500 per contract for agreeing to sell 100 shares of stock at 35 any time up to and including the expiration date. You will have written an in-the-money call because the stock was 36 but the strike price in the call was 35.

After issuing the April 35 call for $500 per contract, three end results are possible:

1. The stock is above 35 at expiration. The stock is called, and you will record a sale at $35 per share *plus* the $5 per share premium that was paid in advance. The total sale price is adjusted to $40 per share *less* the commission paid to write the call and to buy and sell the stock.

2. The stock is below 35 at expiration. You will own the stock and will record a profit earned (in the year of expiration) of $500 per contract less the option commission to write the call. You can then continue to hold the stock, to sell the stock, or to issue another call.

3. You terminate the option obligation through an offsetting purchase.

*Other expiration months, as well as different premiums, would also be available. The April expiration selection was chosen just to simplify the illustration.

If you choose to deliver the 26 cost as a result of a call exercise at 35, you will have a taxable gain of $9 per share *plus* the option premium of $5 per share, which leaves a total gain of $14 per share less all commission costs. *The gain is recorded in the year of the option exercise.*

However, you are not obligated to deliver the 26 cost stock. If you wish to do so, you can instead buy any 100 shares and deliver those. The call is not written against any specific lot of stock.

If XYZ were 40 at the time the call at 35 was exercised, you could buy 100 shares at 40 and deliver those 100 shares against the call exercise. You should instruct the broker buying the new 100 shares to have printed on the purchase confirmation "Vs. Call Exercise at 35," which identifies the new shares as the ones being sold through the call exercise. If that strategy is followed, the following apply:

- The low-cost stock at 26 per share would be retained.
- The new stock bought at 40 would be sold by the call exercise at 35 plus the $5 premium.
- Instead of reporting a taxable gain of $1,400 less commission, a loss would be reported equaling the commissions to buy and sell the stock and write the call.

Investors owning low-cost shares who wish to write calls for income augmentation often fear being called and thus creating large taxable gains. Such investors can rest a little easier with the knowledge that they can control the size of the gain by buying new shares earmarked for delivery against the call exercise. They can also deliver part of the old low-cost shares and buy some new shares, thereby raising their average cost and lowering the recorded gain on a call exercise.

When you wrote the April 35 call with the stock price at 36, you would have written an in-the-money call. This would accomplish the following:

- *Restrict the profit potential* from your cost basis (26) to 35, plus the $5 premium, less commissions.
- *Lower the downside risk* in the stock from 36 (current price) by $5 per share.
- *Bear all the stock ownership risk* from 31 down.

If you did not get called at expiration because the stock was under 35, you could do one of the following:

- Write another call at the same or different strike and for a different term.

- Continue to hold the stock.
- Sell the stock.

Any one of those decisions would have to be tempered by your judgment of the stock and its potential at the expiration of the April 35 call. *Covered call writing is not as simple as many advocates make it out to be!* It is a procedure best suited to investors who are percentage-minded individuals, decision makers, and excellent recordkeepers, willing to limit profit potential and able to understand and accept the risks of stock ownership and of seeking income augmentation.

Cost Basis Approximating the Market.   Stock XYZ is at 35. You bought shares at 35. In early January, you can write XYZ April calls as follows:

Strike Price	Option Price
35	4
40	2
45	1

If you write an April 35 call for $400, you will have written an at-the-market call. *At-the-market* means that the strike price for the call is the same as, or closely approximates, the current market price of the stock. By writing an at-the-market call:

- You have agreed to sell shares at 35 that you bought at 35.
- Your only profit potential (in addition to any cash dividends) comes from the advance premium of $400. The premium profit is sharply lessened by stock and option commissions.
- You must bear all the stock risk from 31 down in return for accepting the advance premium.

To some investors the premium of $400 (representing over 11% immediate cash less the option commission) for approximately three months of obligation can look very attractive. And indeed it is—until the stock gets called. If the stock is sold at 35 versus a call exercise at 35, the gross premium of $400 is sharply reduced by commissions to buy the stock, to write the call, and to sell the stock. Undiscounted commissions at a full-service brokerage firm for 100 shares bought at 35, for one call written at 4, and for 100 shares sold at 35 would approximate $200. Approximately half of the premium received would be eroded by commissions. If called, the investor would still show an approximate 6% net return for the approximate three-month period. If not called, the investor would have earned $400 per contract less the option commission.

If the investor had bought 1,000 shares at 35 and wrote 10 April 35 calls at 4 and was called, the percentage of the commission impact on the total premium received would be substantially less. Undiscounted commissions at a full-service brokerage firm for 1,000 shares bought at 35, for 10 calls written at 4, and for 1,000 shares sold at 35 would approximate $1,200. That total for commissions would approximate 30% of the $4,000 premium received (10 calls × $400). That brings up two very important points for active covered call writers.

1. Getting commission discounts is integral to the success of the activity.
2. Larger orders reduce the commission cost per option and per 100 shares of stock.

Cost Basis Higher than the Market.   Stock XYZ is at 36. You originally bought the shares at 38. In early January, you can write XYZ April calls as follows:

Strike Price	Option Price
35	5
40	2^{1}/$_{4}$
45	1

If you write an April 40 call for 2^{1}/$_{4}$, you will have written an out-of-the-money call. *Out-of-the-money* means that the call strike price of 40 is higher than the current market price of the stock. You bought XYZ at 38 and have experienced a fall in price to 36. In agreeing to sell at 40 (by writing a call), you have done the following:

- *Limited your profit potential* to $2 per share (the difference between your cost and the option strike price), plus the 2^{1}/$_{4}$ per share option premium. If you are called, your total profit (2 + 2^{1}/$_{4}$) will be sharply lessened by commission costs.
- *Reduced the risk* of a further price fall in XYZ by 2^{1}/$_{4}$.
- *Accepted the risk* of a further decline below 33^{3}/$_{4}$.

One reason you might opt for such a low profit potential on the $3,800 investment in XYZ is that you have changed your opinion of XYZ, possibly as a result of a general market decline or a turn for the worse in XYZ's prospects. An immediate sale at 36 versus your cost of 38 would produce a loss aggravated by the commissions.

By writing the out-of-the-money call for $2^1/_4$, you collect some cash to cushion any further decline and retain hope of getting out of XYZ at a profit. You also have the good feeling that you have taken a positive action to help correct a perceived misjudgment.

In the preceding discussions, we have looked at writing calls based on existing holdings of stock. We have also discussed in-the-money calls, at-the-market calls, and out-of-the-money calls. We have also examined writing calls on stock owned with a lower than market cost basis, with a higher than market cost basis, and with a cost basis approximating market price.

The Buy-Write Strategy

Now let's take a careful look at a very common option strategy known in the option world as *buy-write*. This strategy usually involves the investor in purchasing common stock and simultaneously writing calls against the newly purchased shares.

In the buy-write strategy, you can write the call options as in-the-money, at-the-money, or out-of-the-money calls. And not only must you choose strike prices, you must also select expiration months. In selecting strike prices, you must understand that the premiums paid are *highest* for in-the-money calls and *lowest* for out-of-the-money calls. In selecting expiration months, you must also clearly understand that premiums paid when strike prices are equal are *highest* for the most distant month and *lowest* for the nearest month. Keep those understandings firmly in mind while I offer three pieces of advice on the buy-write strategy.

1.   If you are going to buy common shares and immediately write calls, select stocks that you know well and are willing to own as a long-term investment.

2.   Write only out-of-the-money calls. Because you are bearing all the risks of stock ownership, you should retain the possibility of some price appreciation in addition to getting some money in your pocket.

3.   Normally write calls for the middle or the far month of the available expiration months.

Many experienced buy-write option investors concentrate on writing calls for the most distant expiration month for the following reasons:

- For the same strike price, the far month call always provides the greatest amount of premium dollars.
- Writing far month calls lessens the number of decisions and transactions you must make when compared to writing near month calls.
- Fewer transactions means lower commissions to be paid.
- Fewer transactions means less recordkeeping and a simpler tax return.

Some buy-write advocates dwell on writing near-term calls for possible higher annualized returns. These high annualized returns, however, are rarely achieved. Writing near month calls has too many disadvantages for me to recommend it. Among them are the following:

- Relatively small premiums.
- Increased number of decisions to be made.
- Higher commission costs.
- Little downside protection afforded by the premium.

There are sometimes such volatile conditions in a particular market or in a particular stock that writing near month calls may be attractive. This is not the norm, however, and in my opinion, the buy-write investor should concentrate on writing calls for the middle or the far month.

Writing middle month calls normally offers the following:

- High premiums relative to the far month.
- More active markets when compared to volume in the far month.
- Closer spreads between bid and asked prices when compared to the far month.

Do not allow yourself to be mesmerized by the computer-calculated returns that are made available by most large brokerage firms. Buy-write investors often select an opportunity on the basis of *only* a return calculation! That practice can be very dangerous to your financial health. You must always keep the following points in mind:

- It is the stock-owning investor who bears the risk of a stock drop.
- A quarter- or a half-point difference in an option premium will often make a buy-write look attractive from the standpoint of a possible percentage of return, yet offer little extra in downside protection.
- The success or failure of a buy-write depends on stock selection far more than premium collection.

Many experienced buy-write investors consider themselves sophisticated (a label that often precedes a disastrous financial experience) enough to play the execution game. Let me shed some light on how buy-write executions can be obtained. Buy-write investors use four basic methods to establish their desired positions. Let's look carefully at each of these methods using the following stock and option prices:

	Last Price	Bid Price	Asked Price
XYZ stock	35	$34^3/4$	$35^1/4$
XYZ April 35 calls	4	$3^3/4$	$4^1/4$

In early January you decide to execute a buy-write (buy the stock; write the call) strategy on XYZ stock.

Method 1. You instruct your broker to buy XYZ at the market, *paying* the asked price of $35^1/4$. Simultaneously with the stock purchase order, you enter an option order to sell XYZ April 35 calls at the market, *receiving* $3^1/4$. Method 1 is the one most frequently employed by writers of covered calls. Both positions are established quickly and usually in close approximation to the market price at the time the orders are entered.

Method 2. You instruct your broker to buy XYZ at the market, paying the asked price of $35^1/4$. You anticipate a rise in XYZ stock that day, so you delay entering the order to write XYZ April 35 calls. Your hope is that the call price will be higher later in the day (should your judgment of XYZ's upward move prove correct) and that you will be able to *sell calls* for a price higher than the $3^3/4$ *bid price* that was prevailing at the time you purchased your XYZ stock. If your judgment is wrong, you can possibly still sell the XYZ April 35 calls at the same or lower price. You can also decide to hold the stock unoptioned for another day, week, or month, or you can decide not to write calls on XYZ at all. You simply bear the normal risk of stock ownership.

Method 3.   You instruct your broker to write the XYZ April 35 calls at the bid price of $3^3/4$. You delay buying the stock at the asked price of $35^1/4$ because you expect and hope that XYZ will decline during the balance of the day. If your judgment proves to be correct, you may buy XYZ at $34^1/2$, 34, or even lower. If that happens, you have established a buy-write position with a profit potential that is much larger than normal, as well as a nice percentage of downside protection.

The big risk in this situation is that your judgment of XYZ price action during the day may be wrong. The XYZ stock may go up sharply after you have written the call. Maybe XYZ advances to 37 or 38 or even higher. Worse yet, after you have written the call, trading might be halted in XYZ with good news pending concerning a buy-out or an unexpectedly large earnings improvement! News that might send XYZ above 40!

Selling the call first and waiting to buy the stock is the most dangerous of the execution games. The investor is completely "naked" until the stock is bought to "cover" the obligation incurred in writing the call. In my opinion, it is a practice that most investors should avoid.

Method 4.   In this method you place your order to buy XYZ stock and sell XYZ April calls on a *net debit basis*. Net debit basis! Who said writing covered calls was simple?

In this procedure you observe that the last price of the stock is 35 and the last price of the option is 4. You instruct your brokerage firm to buy XYZ and sell the April 35 call at any combination of prices that will result in your account being debited no more than $31 per share (35 stock price minus the 4 option price). If you purchased XYZ at $35^1/4$, you will have to sell the April 35 call for at least $4^1/4$ to produce a net debit of $31 per share. If you purchase XYZ at $34^3/4$, you will have to sell the April 35 call for at least $3^3/4$ to produce a net debit of $31 per share. Strange as it may seem to the uninitiated, the option buyer's premium can be used immediately by the option writer to reduce the cost outlay of the stock being purchased to back (cover) the call written.

In Method 1, when *you execute market orders to buy the stock and write the call,* you are assured of establishing your desired position even though paying the asked price for the stock and receiving the bid price for the option may slightly diminish your return, depending on the last price for the stock and option.

In Method 2, *buying the stock and waiting to write the call option* may increase or decrease your available return, depending on the last price for the stock and option at the time you placed the market order to buy the stock. If, by delaying the execution to sell the call option, you receive more than the last price of the option prevailing at the time you bought the stock, you will have benefited. If the delay in writing the call results in a lower price for the call than that prevailing at the time you bought the stock, you will have lowered your potential return.

In Method 3, you take on the greatest amount of risk by *writing the call first and waiting and hoping for the stock to be lower later in the day.* It certainly is not for the inexperienced or the faint of heart! If you are prone to heart attack or react badly to stress, stay away from this method! Investors who successfully "guess" right and buy stock lower than the prevailing price at the time the option is written obviously "soup up" their potential returns.

In Method 4, by *entering orders on a net debit basis,* you always get executions exactly as you want them—or not at all! Caveat: Not all brokerage firms accept orders on a net debit basis. Generally, it is the larger firms that are equipped to handle this specialized transaction.

Well, now that you have discovered how simple and easy it is to write covered calls, are you ready to begin?

CHAPTER 5

The Sell Stock–
Buy Call Strategy

LOCKING IN PROFIT AND PROFIT POTENTIAL

A common problem for stock owners who have established large unrealized profits in an optionable stock is whether to sell the stock and realize the gain. If they sell the stock and realize the gain and then the stock continues to rise to higher and higher levels, they often feel (despite having realized a profit) either that they were "dumb" in misjudging the stock's potential for further rise or that their emotional need to realize a profit overcame their belief in the stock's potential for additional gain, thereby costing them additional profits.

If they don't sell the stock at the substantial profit afforded by the price rise in the shares, they must bear all of the risk of a downward move in the share price of the stock, a move that could be so sharp and severe as to eradicate completely all the gain, possibly turning their winning position into a losing position.

What a terrible turn of events that would be—a large profit that "gets away" and becomes a large loss! Millions of stock investors, decade after decade, have experienced that terrible scenario of large profit becoming large loss.

WAYS TO STOP THE EROSION OF PROFIT

To reduce the risk of large profits completely eroding or turning into losses, many experienced investors have developed techniques, or systems, to alleviate or to eliminate the possibility. The following three methods are some of the more popular ones used to keep hard-won stock market profits while still retaining upside potential in the winning stock situation.

Method 1. *Sell enough of the winning stock to recover fully all the capital you originally put into the stock, and keep the remainder of the stock in the hope of additional profits.*

Example

You buy 1,000 XYZ at 15. Your total investment is $15,000 plus commission. Stock XYZ advances to 30. You sell 500 XYZ at 30. The proceeds of the sale are $15,000 less commissions. You have now regained all your initial investment (less commission and applicable taxes on the gain, if any).

You keep 500 XYZ in case it rises further, and you have virtually eliminated any possibility of loss that would result from a decline in XYZ's price. You have your original $15,000 back (less commissions) *and* you have 500 shares of XYZ.

Some investors always "book profits" on winning situations, while still retaining an interest in any future price rise, by selling enough shares to guarantee a profit no matter what happens in the future to their stock. Let's use again our example of 1,000 XYZ originally purchased at 15 that rose to 30. If you sell 600 shares at 30, you realize a profit on your initial capital (less commissions), and you still have a future interest in 400 shares of your original holding. You have your original $15,000 back (less commissions), you have 400 shares of XYZ, *and* you have a profit of $3,000 (less taxes).

Method 2. *Place a stop loss order at some point lower than the current market price of the stock.* This practice allows you to retain the entire upside potential in all the shares you own. This certainly sounds good on the surface, and it is often recommended for investor use by brokers and the firms they represent. However, there are just too many problems associated with the stop loss strategy as a profit protector for me to recommend it. Let's examine some of the problems connected with using the stop loss strategy as a profit saver.

• At what percentage level below the current price should the stop be placed? Should you specify 5%, 10%, 15%, or more? There is no right, or always correct, answer. A stock will often dip down low enough to trigger the stop, and then it will snap back, which can make you feel foolish.

• A stop order to sell is an order to sell at the market on the next sale after the stop order is triggered by a sale at the price you have specified in the stop order. In very volatile stocks or very volatile markets, the next price could be way down from the stop price. It could be a price so low that your profit may have disappeared entirely, and there will be a loss on the sale triggered by the stop order.

• Some exchanges will not accept stop orders. Even exchanges that normally do accept stop orders can institute bans on them. Such bans can leave the investor completely exposed to a downside fall in the stock price.

• Placing verbal stop orders with a broker who is in a firm in which stop orders are not permitted or in a firm that has banned them is usually ineffectual. A verbal stop order is really unfair to the broker. The broker trying to watch a stock on a verbal stop order to sell could be out sick, at lunch, or on vacation at the time the stock declines to the verbal stop price. The sell order could go unexecuted, and the profitable situation could turn into a losing situation.

• Using mental stop orders also is laden with problems. Many investors faced with our winning example of 1,000 XYZ bought at 15 and now 30 tell themselves that they will watch the stock. If it goes to 27 (or any selected price that they have decided would be a good exit price), they tell themselves that they will simply call their broker and sell all or part of their 1,000 shares as close as possible to their mental stop price. This method is also very ineffective. If you choose to use it, you must continually monitor the situation. You could be on vacation or sick (or simply unaware) when your mental stop price is reached. By the time you are aware of the drop, a further price fall deep enough to produce a capital loss if you sell shares may have occurred. Mental stops are also too easily changed. You can always to yourself, "I'll give it another point." Or perhaps you give it 2 points below your original mental stop point. You may continue to make lower adjustments to the point at which your entire profit has disappeared and a loss exists.

Method 3. *Sell the entire holding of the winning stock and, simultaneously with the sale of the stock, purchase a call option on the same stock.* This is one of the best and surest profit preservers (that also allows participation in a possible future price rise) for owners of optionable stocks with large *unrealized* capital gains. The purchase of the call option is funded by part of the proceeds of the stock sale. This particular method accomplishes four things:

1. A gain on the stock is realized, that is, locked in.

2. The capital removed from the stock situation is immediately available for reinvestment in another stock(s), bonds, funds, CDs, or whatever you wish. The capital has been freed.

3. No matter what happens to the stock after the sale at a profit, you cannot experience a loss. The risk that you bore as a stock owner has been removed.

4. *Through the call ownership, you keep virtually unlimited upside profit potential should the stock continue to rise after the stock sale and before the option expires.* The amount of upside profit potential retained through your ownership of the call will depend on the number of calls you purchased and the stock prices in the calls.

If you purchase calls to retain upside potential in a profitable optionable stock that you have sold, you can also choose various lengths of time that you wish to retain the upside potential. Let's look carefully at the following example to see some of the possibilities for the investor wishing to maintain an interest in a future price rise in a stock sold at a substantial profit.

Example

You purchased 1,000 XYZ at 25, and XYZ is now 44. In early January, you sell 1,000 XYZ at 44. You realize a $19,000 gain, less commissions to buy and sell and before taxes, if any are required. (Sometimes gains are not taxable as a result of offsetting losses or as a result of the gain being realized in a tax-deferred account such as an IRA.) You want to retain an interest in XYZ should it move higher over the next few months. In January, April XYZ call options are available as follows:

Stock	Strike	Option
44	40	6
	45	3

If you buy 10 XYZ April 40s for 6, you will be investing $6,000 (plus commission) of your $19,000 pretax, precommission gain. The 10 calls entitle you to all the possible price rise in 1,000 shares of XYZ from 40 up. That right extends through the April expiration, or approximately three months after the sale of XYZ at 44. At the April expiration:

- If XYZ is still 44, you can sell the 10 calls at 4, for $4,000 (less commissions), thus recovering approximately two-thirds of the purchase price of the calls.
- If XYZ is below 40, the calls will expire worthless. The loss in a taxable account will be tax deductible from the already realized gains.
- If XYZ is 50, the 10 calls at 40 could be sold for $10,000 (less commissions). You would have earned an additional profit from XYZ's moving upward plus full recovery of the cost of the calls.
- If XYZ is higher than 50, obviously the calls at 40 could be sold for their intrinsic worth (less commissions), producing even bigger gains for you.

If you decide to keep more of your $19,000 realized gain, yet still retain an interest in a future high price for XYZ, you could opt to purchase 10 April 45s at 3. This would involve only $3,000 (plus commission) of your $19,000 realized gain. This call purchase would entitle you to all the possible price rise in 1,000 shares of XYZ above 45. That right would extend through the April expiration, or approximately three months after the sale of XYZ at 44. At the April expiration:

- If XYZ is still 44 (unchanged from the January stock sale price), the calls at 45 will expire *worthless*. Your loss (in a taxable account) would be tax deductible from the already realized gain.
- If XYZ is 50, the 10 calls at 45 could be sold for $5,000 (less commissions). You would have an additional profit from XYZ's upward price move and recover all the $3,000 initially invested in the call purchase.
- If XYZ is higher than 50, obviously you could sell the calls at 45 for their intrinsic worth (less commissions), producing even bigger gains.

Yes, the strategy of selling profitable stock and buying calls with a portion of the profits booked is a frequently employed method of preserving profit and retaining upside profit potential, particularly by that group of investors who have "ridden stocks up and ridden them down" and who now want to hedge their investment somewhat.

In the preceding example, I touched on only two call buying possibilities for using part of the proceeds of a profitable stock sale: (1) A purchase of in-the-money calls (stock price 44; call strike price 40), and (2) a purchase of out-of-the-money calls (stock price 44; call strike price 45).

Once you have sold a profitable share holding and made the decision to reinvest part of your profits into call options, you must cope with certain variables, such as the following:

- The amount of profit to invest in call options.
- The strike price(s) in the calls.
- The expiration months for the calls.
- The quantity of calls to purchase.

Those judgments are normally influenced by your attitude and feeling toward the outlook for possible further appreciation in the stock.

Whatever your choice, the goals of *realizing profits, preventing capital loss,* and *retaining an interest in an XYZ upmove for a period* after *the stock sale* would have been maintained. Your worry and stress over any possible large percentage of decline in XYZ would have been eliminated. As someone once said, "Try it! You'll like it!" Booking some or all of the profit from a rise in stock price while retaining substantial upside potential by means of a call purchase makes for happier investing.

CHAPTER 6

Buying Puts on Owned Stock to Preserve Profit and Limit Risk

Earlier chapters have discussed a frequent problem encountered by stock investors: how to go about preserving a profitable rise in the share price while still retaining an interest in a future price rise. As has been discussed, you have several choices available when you seek to preserve part or all of the gain resulting from a fortuitous stock selection, as follows:

- Selling enough of the stock to regain the original capital invested in the total position and retaining the balance for possible further appreciation.

- Selling the entire position, and with part of the profit, buying call options on the same stock to participate in a possible further rise in price.

- Placing a stop loss order (where permitted) at some chosen percentage below the current price of the stock.

In addition to wishing to prevent a hard-won stock market profit from possibly eroding away, the winning investor also often desires to retain part or all of a possible future rise in price of the shares owned. Buying puts on profitable stock positions is a popular method used by many sophisticated investors who seek to preserve profits while keeping intact the unlimited upside profit potential in the stock.

THE ADVANTAGES AND DISADVANTAGES
OF BUYING PUT OPTIONS

Buying At-the-Market Puts on Profitable Stock

You have purchased 1,000 shares of XYZ at 20, and the stock has risen to 45. You are nervous about the market. You still believe XYZ may rise still further, but you want to nail down your profit. In early January, the put prices on XYZ for April are as follows:

Strike Price	Put Option Price
45	2
50	6

You can easily calm your nerves and allay the fear of a substantial price fall in XYZ by acquiring 10 XYZ April 45 puts at 2. To do so, you will have to make a cash outlay of $2,000 (10 x $200), plus the option commission. The put purchase provides insurance for you so that you can sell the 1,000 shares at any time from the January put purchase date to the April expiration date (approximately three months) for 45 per share, less the stock sales commission.

If XYZ plummets all the way back to the purchase price of 20, you are still assured that you can sell your 1,000 shares at 45! The put premium of $2,000 will be a loss and can be viewed like any insurance premium paid to protect an asset against loss or destruction. With the premium paid for the right to sell (put) the 1,000 shares at 45, you can rest easy about the market while the put is in effect. The bulk of the profit has been absolutely retained!

If XYZ continues to advance in price after the acquisition of the put, you participate in that further rise. If XYZ is 60 at the April expiration of the put, you can then decide to do one of the following:

• Sell the stock at 60, realizing a much larger profit than was available in January at the time of the put purchase. The profit on a sale at 60 would be lessened by the loss of $2,000 in the expired put.

• Keep the stock and acquire a new put at the 60 strike price, recording as a loss the $2,000 premium paid for the April 45 put. That premium loss would be regained through the new put exercise when the stock is sold at 60 or at a price higher than 60.

Put owners do not have to wait for the expiration of their put to take action. If XYZ has sharply declined after the put purchase and you view any substantial recovery above the put price as highly improbable, you can exercise the put at 45. This will free up $45,000 (less the stock commission and less the total cost of the put) to reinvest as you choose.

If XYZ has risen sharply before the put expiration, you can sell the stock at the new higher price and (1) retain the now out-of-the-money put at 45 for a hoped-for profit on a price collapse of XYZ below 45 before the expiration of the put, or (2) sell the put for whatever value is available, thereby recovering some part of the original premium you paid for the put.

Buying In-the-Money Puts on Profitable Stock

As in the previous illustration, you have purchased 1,000 XYZ at 20, and it has risen to 45. You are nervous about the market. You believe that XYZ may rise still further, but you want to make certain of your profit. In early January, the put prices on XYZ for April are as follows:

Strike Price	Put Option Price
45	2
50	6

Here, you have two choices (there are normally many choices available because of different expiration months and different strike prices) readily available to insure that the bulk of your hard-won profit is protected, while you still participate in a future price increase in XYZ that may occur.

1. If, as in the illustration of buying at-the-market puts, you buy 10 XYZ April 45 puts for 2, you have an immediate capital outlay of $2,000, plus commission. This outlay protects the profit to the $45 level and allows for additional profits should XYZ advance and remain over 45 by the April expiration. *You risk the entire loss of the $2,000 put premium in order to protect the profit.* That appears to be a reasonable avenue to pursue, not only in this example but in the real world of investing.

2. Another avenue for your consideration is to purchase in-the-money puts at 50 for 6. With XYZ at 45, the in-the-money puts at 50 are available with very little "time premium." Buying 10 XYZ April 50 puts at 6 involves a capital outlay of $6,000, plus the option commission. *That amount would*

be three times the amount required to buy 10 at-the-market puts with a 45 strike price!

You may readily wonder why you might choose the higher-strike-price (50), higher-cost puts ($6,000) over the lower-strike-price (45), lower-cost puts ($2,000). Let's look at a line of reasoning that *might* lead you to choose the higher-priced puts. (Commissions are omitted for the sake of simplicity of illustration in the following examples.)

Example 1

In January XYZ is 45	In April XYZ is 25
A. Buy 10 April 45 puts for $2,000	Sell 1,000 XYZ @ 45 by exercise of put. You realize $43,000 after deducting the put cost.
B. Buy 10 April 50 puts for $6,000	Sell 1,000 XYZ @ 50 by exercise of put. You realize $44,000 after deducting the put cost.

Example 2

In January XYZ is 45	In April XYZ is 60
A. Buy 10 April puts for $2,000	Buy 1,000 XYZ @ 60.10 April 45 puts expire worthless, and you lose the $2,000 premium. You realize $58,000 after deducting the put cost.
B. Buy 10 April 50 puts for $6,000	Sell 1,000 XYZ @ 60. 10 April 50 puts expire worthless, and you lose the $6,000 premium. You realize $54,000 after deducting the put cost.

On a sharp move down in the stock, the buyer of in-the-money puts fares better than does the buyer of at-the-market puts. *On a sharp move up* in the stock, the converse is true. The buyer of in-the-money puts fares *much worse* than the buyer of at-the-market puts.

To get an even clearer picture of the two protective put purchases in the preceding examples, carefully review Tables 6.1 and 6.2, which show various possible results at the April expiration. In each case, the January price of XYZ is 45.

Table 6.1   Example of Results 45 Puts

1,000 XYZ Bought @ 20	10 XYZ April 45 Puts Bought for $2,000		
Possible Prices of XYZ at April 45 Put Expiration	Proceeds of 1,000 XYZ Sold	April 45 Put Option Cost	Pretax Precommission Profit
25	$45,000	$2,000[a]	$23,000
35	45,000	2,000[a]	23,000
45	45,000	2,000[a]	23,000
55	55,000	2,000[b]	33,000
65	65,000	2,000[b]	43,000

[a]Puts exercised.
[b]Puts expire worthless.

Table 6.2   Example of Results 50 Puts

1,000 XYZ Bought @ 20	10 XYZ April 50 Puts Bought for $6,000		
Possible Prices of XYZ at April 50 Put Expiration	Proceeds of 1,000 XYZ Sold	April 50 Put Option Cost	Pretax Precommission Profit
25	$50,000	$6,000[a]	$24,000
35	50,000	6,000[a]	24,000
45	50,000	6,000[a]	24,000
55	55,000	6,000[b]	29,000
65	65,000	6,000[b]	39,000

[a]Puts exercised.
[b]Puts expire worthless.

As you can see from Table 6.1, $23,000 of January's available $25,000 profit was completely "insured" by the put purchase, and the investor retained unlimited upside potential for the life of the put.

As Table 6.2 shows, $24,000 of January's available profit was completely "insured" by the put purchase. The unlimited upside potential in XYZ was retained for the life of the put.

For most investors, the much higher cost of the in-the-money puts precludes their purchase as insurance when at-the-money puts are available at a low cost similar to those shown in Examples 1 and 2.

The disadvantages of in-the-money put purchases as a protection of stock profits while seeking additional upside gains are the following:

- Higher cash outlay is required for the higher-priced puts.
- There is a reduced profit potential on a substantial upside move in XYZ when compared to the at-the-market put.

The only real advantage of the in-the-money put purchase over the at-the-market put purchase (in the same expiration month) in protecting a profitable stock holding is the reduction in the amount of the put insurance lost should the put be exercised when the stock is priced at or below the exercise price in an at-the-market put.

Many well-informed option investors also buy puts on profitable stock holdings with the intent of transferring a profit into a different tax year. Their focus is not on any additional upside potential that the stock may have but on minimizing the tax consequences caused by a profitable stock sale. Of course, any additional gains that are realized as a byproduct of the put purchase are welcomed. Because investors' focus is on profit protection rather than profit enhancement, they often buy the put that will produce the least loss of the put premium should the stock decline.

Example 3

You buy 1,000 XYZ at 15. In early October, XYZ is at 45. If you sell at 45, you will realize a $30,000 gain. If you do not sell in October but try to wait until January to sell and place the gain into a different tax year, XYZ may decline substantially from the 45 level. Your gain could be eradicated, and you could possibly incur a loss.

Buying January XYZ puts insures you of a profitable gain to realize in January. The put that would be the least expensive in terms of preserving profit and minimizing put premium loss would be the in-the-money put.

Let's assume XYZ is at 45. In early October you check the price of XYZ January puts. They are quoted as follows:

Strike Price	Put Option Price
45	2
50	6

With your focus on downside protection with the smallest premium loss (versus a sale at 45), you may very well buy 10 XYZ Jan 50s at 6. In January you will exercise the puts if XYZ is below 50 or sell XYZ shares at the market if XYZ is higher than 50.

The profit (less any put premium loss) has been neatly and effectively transferred from one tax year to another! You have kept your peace of mind and alleviated worry over an XYZ price fall between October and January. Table 6.3 should clarify the strategy. In Table 6.3, you originally bought XYZ at 15. You now buy 10 XYZ Jan 50 puts for $6,000. The October price of XYZ is at 45. (Commissions are omitted to simplify illustration.)

As can be seen in Table 6.3, the true cost of your put insurance on the exercised puts when compared against an October sale at 45 was $1,000, plus the option commission. In return for that insurance, you achieved the following:

- Obtained unlimited upside profit potential from the October put purchase date to the January put expiration date.
- Effected the transfer of a large profit from one tax year to another tax year.
- Relieved yourself from worry over a price drop in XYZ from October to January.

Even the *most conservative* of investors might find this strategy suitable for particular profitable stock holdings.

Table 6.3   Example of Results

Possible January Prices of XYZ	Sale Proceeds of 1,000 XYZ	January 50 Put Option Cost[a]	Pretax Precommission Profit
N/A	$45,000		$30,000
25	45,000	$6,000[b]	20,000
35	50,000	6,000[b]	29,000
45	50,000	6,000[b]	29,000
55	55,000	6,000[c]	34,000
65	65,000	6,000[c]	44,000

[a]If sold in October.
[b]Puts exercised.
[c]Puts expire worthless.

USING PUTS TO PROTECT NEWLY BOUGHT STOCKS

Another strategic use of put purchases is to insure newly purchased stock shares. This strategy of simultaneous stock purchase and protective put purchase is often highly advocated by retail brokerage firms seeking to substantially increase their commission revenues. In my view, the strategy of simultaneously purchasing stocks and puts primarily benefits only two entities: (1) the brokerage firm and (2) the account executive—although it is widely heralded as a strategy to limit and contain an investor's stock risk.

Let's examine the strategy through my eyes, however. Perhaps then you will see why I believe the simultaneous stock purchase—put purchase strategy increases investor risk when compared to an outright call purchase!

Look carefully at the following illustrations. Their rationale might help you better understand comparative option strategies and perhaps save you hundreds or thousands of dollars during your investing lifetime.

Simultaneous Stock Purchase–Put Purchase

Let's say that you are attracted to XYZ common stock priced at 45. The market and the stock are volatile. In spite of the volatility, you believe that XYZ can advance sharply over the next six months. Despite your belief, you wish to limit your loss potential to a fixed predetermined amount. In early January the option quotations for July puts are as follows:

Strike Price	Put Option Price
45	4

You execute the simultaneous stock purchase–put purchase strategy by doing the following:

Buying 1,000 XYZ @ 45	$45,000
Paying full-service commission	590
Buying 10 XYZ July 45 puts @ 4	4,000
Paying full-service commission	153
Total outlay	$49,743

At any price 45 or below, you lose $5,333, according to the results shown in Table 6.4. This $5,333 is the loss of the put premium plus the commissions to buy and to sell the stock *plus* the option commission. In addition, you lose any difference between the dividend (if any) paid while you owned the stock as well as what the original $45,000 could have safely earned in Treasury bills or a money market fund. Commission costs could be reduced by negotiating a discount through a full-service firm or dealing with a discount firm.

For suffering the expense of the put premiums and the put commission as well as "guaranteeing" the expenditure of commissions to buy and to sell 1,000 XYZ, all that you could gain from an upside move in XYZ *would be the profit possibility* above 50. A sale at 50 at expiration would simply allow you to regain the money invested in the stock and the put option and commissions. You would still be a loser of the amount of interest that could have been earned above any dividend receipt.

If at July expiration you wanted to continue to own the 1,000 XYZ (assuming that XYZ is above 45 with puts expiring worthless), you could do so. However, you would have to do one of the following:

- Pay another put premium and commission to remain protected.
- Go unprotected and run the risk of a severe price decline in XYZ.

If you are sufficiently risk-conscious to have purchased the puts in the initial commitment to XYZ, you may not consider either of these alternatives to be attractive.

Table 6.4   Possible Outcomes of Stock Purchase–
Put Purchase at July Expiration

XYZ Possible Prices	Put Cost and Stock Cost with Commission to Buy	Proceeds of Stock Sold with Commission to Sell	Net Profit (Loss)
35	$49,743	$44,410[a]	($5,333)
45	49,743	44,410[a]	(5,333)
55	49,743	54,350[b]	4,603
65	49,743	64,290[b]	14,547

[a]Puts exercised.
[b]Puts expire worthless.

Call Option Purchase

Now let's look at Table 6.5, which depicts an alternate method of seeking upside potential in that same XYZ stock through purchasing a call option purchase. Say that you are attracted to XYZ priced at 45. Rather than buying 1,000 XYZ at 45 and simultaneously purchasing puts at 45 to limit and contain the risk, in early January you get quotations on July call options.

Strike Price	Call Option Price
45	4

You buy 10 XYZ July 45 calls at 4, with a total cost as follows:

Buying 10 XYZ July 45 calls @ 4	$4,000
Paying full-service option commission	153
Total outlay	$4,153

In comparing the Table 6.4 strategy of buying stock/buying puts with the Table 6.5 strategy of simply buying calls, you can readily ascertain why I suggest that buying calls is the much more viable strategy.

If XYZ declines sharply from the 45 level, at expiration the call buyer would lose less than the owner of the stock and the puts. If XYZ advances from the 45 price, the call buyer makes more money than the owner of the stock and the puts!

Table 6.5 Possible Outcomes of XYZ July 45 Call Option Purchase at July Expiration

XYZ Possible Prices	Call Option Cost with Commission	Proceeds of Option Sale Less Option Commission	Net Profit (Loss)
35	$4,153	0[a]	($4,153)
45	4,153	0[a]	(4,153)
55	4,153	$ 9,778	5,625
65	4,153	19,666	15,510

[a]Expires worthless.

And that's not all. The money *not* invested in the stock ($45,000 plus commission per our example) could be earning interest in money market funds or similar liquid investments.

An ancient philosopher once observed, "Beauty is in the eyes of the beholder." And so it is when it comes to certain option strategies.

Most brokerage firms, their account executives, and compliance officers view buying stock and simultaneously buying puts as insurance, as a *conservative investment practice*. They also view the outright purchase of calls as *highly speculative*. From reading the preceding discussion, you should be able to determine that "it ain't necessarily so!"

CHAPTER 7

Straddle Writing for the Conservative Investor

To the uninitiated, the term *straddle writing* is even more mysterious and confusing than other more familiar argot of the option world, such as puts and calls. Through continuous advertising and public education by the various option exchanges and their brokerage firm members, millions of investors have gained at least *some* understanding of how puts and calls are used in simple investment strategies. The understanding of most investors is usually oriented to the straightout purchase of puts and calls. Buying either puts or calls to seek large potential gains with a predetermined, finite, and limited risk is usually the option strategy first attempted by most investors. This bias toward purchasing puts or calls is quite easy to understand because it requires only a small amount of capital to test the strategy, it offers a high degree of leverage, and it offers very high profit potential.

As you have learned from earlier chapters, writing puts and calls is a much more difficult concept for most investors to comprehend. Getting into and out of various option writing positions is characterized by the following:

- It is often very complex because it involves both the stock and the option markets.
- The capital requirements for writing options are substantially greater than for buying options.
- The potential for profits for option writers is limited.
- The risk of loss is greater than the potential for gain.

Despite the foregoing apparent deterrents, hundreds of thousands of investors have become participants in the writing of puts and calls. They are drawn most often to writing call options against underlying stock shares that they own.

Adherents to covered call writing often issue their contracts for a great variety of reasons, among which are the following:

- To reduce somewhat the risk inherent in stock ownership.
- To achieve cash flow that substantially augments any cash dividends due them as share owners.
- To attempt to achieve an overall rate of return on the total capital invested in their stocks that would be significantly higher than that which could be readily obtained in Treasury bills.

Once you have become experienced in writing stock covered calls and feel comfortable in the various strategies and the overall results obtained, you may cast an eye toward other more sophisticated option writing strategies, such as straddle writing.

Straddle writing is an option strategy that involves the *issuance* of both a put and a call on the same underlying stock when (1) the strike prices in the put and the call are the same and (2) the expiration dates in the put and the call are identical.

Conservative investors who engage in writing straddles always own at least the number of underlying shares, or securities, necessary to deliver in the event the call portion of the straddle is exercised. They also reserve funds to completely pay for any shares or securities that they could be forced to buy as a result of a put exercise.

The reasons many conservative investors write straddles are many and varied. The most prominent reasons for writing straddles with the calls backed by stock ownership and the puts backed by full cash reserves are to earn very high returns on capital and to acquire a desired stock for less than the current price at the time the straddle is written.

Let's take a look now at some specific illustrations involving a conservative investor who is issuing straddles. For the purposes of our illustration, let's assume that you are our investor and that you have carefully researched XYZ and decided that you are willing to accept the risk of owning 1,000 shares.

- The current market price of XYZ is 25.
- XYZ July 25 calls are priced at 3 in early January.
- XYZ July 25 puts are priced at 3 in early January.
- XYZ pays quarterly dividends at 0.20 per share.

Example 1

One course of action you could take would be simply to buy and pay for 1,000 XYZ at 25. Bearing all the downside risk and becoming a participant in the unlimited profit potential above 25, you would be immediately out the stock commission expense and dependent on your correct judgment to produce a profit eventually.

Another course of action would be to buy 500 XYZ at 25 and issue 5 July puts at 3 each and 5 July calls at 3 each. Let's examine Table 7.1 to get a clearer outlook on some possible outcomes of the straddle writing adventure.

The possibility of XYZ being exactly 25 at the July expiration and of both the puts and the calls expiring unexercised is quite unlikely. If that did happen, it would obviously benefit the writer of the puts and the calls.

On being called (Outcome A in Table 7.1), you have total cash available to reinvest of $27,906, which is your original starting capital plus earnings. You have a wide variety of reinvestment choices, such as the following:

- You can write puts on XYZ if you still favor that stock.
- You can rebuy some shares of XYZ and issue straddles against the new shares.
- You can reinvest in a different stock and write calls or straddles against the new shares.

After Outcome B (Table 7.1), you own the 1,000 shares of XYZ that you were willing to risk owning in January when the stock was priced at 25. You are ahead $3,416, and you can choose among the following:

- You can sell the shares if your opinion of XYZ has changed, thereby diminishing the earnings of $3,416 by any amount of loss that is acceptable to you.
- You can hold the shares unoptioned for future appreciation or for future call writing.
- You can write 10 new call options at the same 25 strike if possible, thereby collecting additional premium to lessen any further downside risk and to enhance the overall return on your investment. When you buy 500 XYZ at 25 and write 5 July 25 straddles as opposed to buying 1,000 XYZ and holding it unoptioned for whatever appreciation might occur, you are simply making a trade-off. You are accepting a large number of dollars paid cash in advance as protection against a downward movement in 500 XYZ

Table 7.1   Buy 500 XYZ at 25 and Write 5 July 25 Straddles

On January 15 XYZ is 25		Possible Outcomes at July 15 Expiration[a]	
Buys 500 XYZ @ 25	$12,500	A.	*XYZ above 25.* 5 July 25 puts expire worthless. 5 July 25 calls will be exercised and 500 XYZ sold for $12,245 (commission included).
Plus full-service			
commission	+255		
Net stock cost	$12,755		
			Net loss on stock sold −$ 510
			Net profit on options 2,834
Sell 5 July 25 calls @ 3	$ 1,500		Net profit $2,324
Sell 5 July 25 puts @ 3	+1,500		Two dividends received +200
	$ 3,000		Interest earnings on
Less full-service			$12,755 put reserve @ 6% +382
commissions	−166		Net earnings on total
Net profit on options	$ 2,834		capital $2,906
You maintain interest-earning cash reserve of $12,755 to pay for 500 XYZ if puts exercised.		B.	*XYZ below 25.* 5 July 25 calls expire worthless. 5 July 25 puts exercised and 500 XYZ bought @ 25 = $12,755 (commission included).
			You now own 1,000 XYZ at a net cost of $25,510.
			Earnings from net option
			premium $2,834
			Dividends earned +200
			Interest earnings on put
			reserves +382
			Total net earnings $3,416

[a]The possibility of XYZ being exactly 25 at July expiration and both the puts and the calls expiring unexercised is quite remote. If that did happen, it would obviously benefit the writer of the puts and calls.

by July. That position can be compared to no protection against risk in 1,000 XYZ with unlimited profit potential. Trading a positive bird in the hand for what might be two in the bush makes sense to an awful lot of conservative investors.

Example 2

Again using for illustration the prices used for Table 7.1, how does buying 500 XYZ at 25 and writing 5 XYZ July 25 calls at 3 and 5 XYZ July 25 puts at 3 compare with buying 1,000 XYZ at 25 and simply issuing 10 July 25 calls at 3? See Table 7.2 for this comparison.

In comparing the results of Table 7.2 to those of Table 7.1, you should notice that the writer of the covered straddle nets considerably more dollars than does the writer of the covered call if the stock is above 25 at July expiration. The extra earnings result from the following:

- Lower commission expense on purchase of the stock.
- Greater interest earnings.
- The put premium portion of the straddle.

Table 7.2   Buy 1,000 XYZ at 25 and Write 10 XYZ July 25 Calls at 3

On January 15 XYZ is 25		Possible Outcomes at July Expiration	
Buy 1,000 XYZ @ 25	$25,000	A.	XYZ *above 25.* 10 July 25 calls will be
Plus full-service			exercised and 1,000 XYZ sold for
commission	+453		$24,547 (commission included).
Net stock cost	$25,453		
		Net loss on stock sale	−$ 906
		Net profit on option	2,858
Sell 10 XYZ		Net profit	$1,952
July 25 calls @ 3	$ 3,000	Two dividends received	+400
Less full-service			$2,352
commission	−142	Interest earnings on option	
Net profit on option	$ 2,858	premium received in	
		advance @ 6%	+85
		New earnings on total capital	$2,437
		B.	XYZ *below 25.* 10 July 25 calls expire worthless.
		You now own 1,000 XYZ with a net cost of $25,453.	
		Earnings from net option	
		premium	$2,858
		Dividends earned	+400
		Interest earnings on option	
		premium	+85
		Total net earnings	$3,343

You will also see that the writer of the straddle nets only slightly more than does the writer of the covered call when the stock is below 25 at the July expiration. The small additional earnings are primarily a result of interest earnings on capital reserved for the put exercise.

The lesson to be learned from these comparisons is that when put premiums are relatively equal to call premiums and when you are an option writer contemplating buying stock and issuing covered calls, you will do better if you buy one-half of the contemplated share purchase and issue covered straddles (assuming the contemplated share purchase is divisible by 2 and that the result would be in round lots of 100 shares).

Once you have made the decision to issue straddles with the calls backed by the required securities and reserves available to meet any put exercise, you should give some thought to actions that you might take during the life of the straddle.

Some issuers of straddles adopt the do-nothing philosophy. They issue straddles and do nothing until:

- Both the puts and the calls expire unexercised.
- The calls are exercised and the puts expire.
- The puts are exercised and the calls expire.

Most experienced straddle writers tend to plan certain actions that they can implement early in the life of their straddle obligation in the event of a sharp increase or sharp decline in the price of the underlying stock.

Let's suppose that in early January you buy 500 XYZ at 25 and issue 5 July 25 puts at 3, and that you also issue 5 July 25 calls at 3. Look carefully at the following two scenarios.

Scenario 1: In Early February XYZ Rises to 32.   With XYZ at 32, the right to put (sell) the stock at 25 until the July expiration will have declined substantially from the price of 3 in January when XYZ was only 25.

Puts on a 25 stock 7 points out of the money, even with five months' life, would have only a minimum value in the market place. That value would normally be a small fraction, such as $3/8$ to $1/4$. The experienced straddle writer often buys offsetting out-of-the-money options that have substantial remaining life when the offsetting purchase can be made for a small fraction of the original option sale price. In our scenario, you could cancel out your July 25 put obligation by purchasing 5 July 25 puts at $3/8$ or less.

Should XYZ decline substantially from the February 32 level after the July 25 put obligation was relieved, you could again issue July 25 puts and collect a much larger premium than that paid to cancel out your initial obligation.

This purchase and reissue of July 25 puts would necessarily depend on wide rises and falls in XYZ's price. It is not an infrequent occurrence for a straddle writer to be able to cancel out an obligation through an offsetting purchase and to reissue the share obligation several times during the life of the straddle. Each reissuance at a much higher price than the canceling purchase simply adds more dollars in the investor's pocket.

Certainly the writer of the straddle has to be:

- Cognizant of wide price moves in the underlying stock on which he or she has straddle obligations.
- Cognizant of price changes of the straddle parts.
- Cognizant of the remaining life in the straddle obligations.
- Prepared to take action when most of the profit potential in a straddle leg has been obtained.

Scenario 2: In Early February XYZ Drops to 18.   With XYZ at 18, the right to call (buy) the stock at 25 until the July expiration will have declined substantially from the price of 3 in January when XYZ was only 25. Calls on a 25 stock 7 points out of the money, even with five months' life, would have only a minimum value in the marketplace. That value would normally be a small fraction, such as $3/8$ to $1/4$.

Just as in Scenario 1, the experienced writer of straddles would most likely make a call purchase at a small fraction to offset the obligation to deliver shares at 25 until the July expiration.

Should XYZ rally substantially in price after the call obligation was canceled through an offsetting purchase, you might again be able to write July 25 calls for a sum much greater than what you spent to purchase the calls that canceled out the initial obligation.

If XYZ continued to rally and decline, the alert straddle writer might be able to purchase offsetting calls at low prices several times before the July expiration and to reissue July 25 calls at high prices. Each reissuance at a much higher price than the canceling purchase simply adds more dollars in the investor's pocket.

WARNING

Writing straddles with the call portion backed by the required securities and the put portion backed by cash reserves is an investment strategy that should be undertaken only by the following:

- Investors who are informed and knowledgeable about the underlying stock.
- Investors who are well versed in option strategy.
- Investors who are good recordkeepers.
- Investors who are decision makers and who enjoy the hands-on management required of straddle writers.

CHAPTER 8

Selling Puts Backed by 100% Cash Reserves

As has been discussed in earlier chapters, many informed and self-labeled conservative investors attempt to earn a high return on their investment capital through the issuance of call options that are completely collateralized by ownership of the underlying stock or securities. Not only do individuals in large numbers attempt to earn high returns through covered call writing but so do an ever-increasing number of institutional investors, such as mutual funds, pension plans, banks, and insurance companies.

Many of these participants in call option writing are often drawn to substituting writing puts that are 100% backed by Treasury bills (T-bills) or other liquid money reserves, as a viable alternative to writing stock-backed calls. In fact, many sophisticated and knowledgeable investors in the option market consider writing at-the-market puts that are backed 100% with cash reserves to be superior to writing at-the-market covered calls.

In this chapter, we discuss why some market sophisticates focus on writing puts and the defensive strategies they use when adverse price moves occur in stocks. There are two main reasons why investors engage in regular programs of put writing: (1) to earn a high return on capital, and (2) to possibly acquire favored stocks at prices below the prevailing price(s) at the time the put is issued.

When put premiums approximate call premiums on a specific stock at the same strike price and for the same expiration month, writing puts that are backed by cash reserves is a far superior strategy to buying the stock and issuing covered calls!

The following examples should help you to see clearly the advantages of at-the-market put writing versus at-the-market call writing that is backed by stock.

Example 1

Assume that XYZ in mid-February is 25 per share. You like XYZ at the current level despite the low yield from the $0.80 annual dividend, but you wish to gain some downside risk protection from an acceptance of option premium. The mid-February options quotations for XYZ are the following:

Expiration Month	Strike Price	Calls	Puts
June	25	3	3

If you are contemplating ownership of 1,000 XYZ, you could buy 1,000 shares at 25 and write 10 XYZ June 25 calls. Table 8.1 shows the net results if the calls were exercised at the end of the period as a result of XYZ being higher than 25.

As the investor in Table 8.1, you bore all the downside risk in XYZ to

Table 8.1   The Covered Call Writer's Risk and Reward

In February XYZ is 25		In June XYZ is above 25	
Buy 1,000 XYZ @ 25	$25,000	Sell 1,000 XYZ @ 25 via call	
Plus full-service		exercise	$25,000
commission	+453	Less full-service commission	−453
Net stock cost	$25,453	Net profit on options	$24,547
Sell 10 XYZ June 25			
calls @ 3	$ 3,000		
Less full-service			
commission	−142		
Net option proceeds	$ 2,858		
Net stock cost	$25,453		
Net option proceeds	−2,858		
Net capital at risk	$22,595		

Net gain on transactions	$1,952	($24,547 − $22,595)	
Dividends earned	+200		
Total net earnings	$2,152		

the June expiration in return for the advance premium plus the cash dividends paid by XYZ. Your maximum profit after commission expenses (at a full-service firm) was $2,152. That amount would have represented a pretax return of 9.5% on the $22,595 out-of-pocket capital you initially invested and would certainly be considered an excellent return for the period by almost any measurement. And you could have enhanced the return through the negotiation of commission discounts.

Example 2

Now compare the risk and reward potential shown in Table 8.1 to that shown in Table 8.2, where you collateralize the issued puts with Treasury bills yielding 6% annually.

The profit comparisons of the outcomes in Table 8.1 and Table 8.2 are dramatically different!

Table 8.2 The Put Writer's Risk and Reward

In February XYZ is 25		In June XYZ is above 25	
Sell 10 XYZ June 25		10 XYZ June 25 puts expire	
puts @ 3	$ 3,000	25M T-bills redeemed	$25,000
Less full-service			
commission	−142		
Net put proceeds	$ 2,858		
Buy 25M Treasury bills	$25,000		
Plus full-service			
commission	+60		
Net T bill cost	$25,060		
Net option proceeds	−2,858		
Net capital invested	$22,202		
Net gain on transactions	$2,798	($25,000 − $22,202)	
Interest earnings on			
T-bills for 4 months	+500[a]		
Total net earnings	$3,298		

[a]In reality the T-bill interest earnings would be reflected in a purchase price at a discount. For purposes of simplification of interest computation, the purchase was shown at face value.

	Out-of-Pocket Capital	Net Profit Pretax if XYZ over 25 at Expiration
Stock-covered calls	$22,595	$2,152
T-bill backed puts	22,202	3,298

In each case, you incurred on the options you wrote an equal risk of a down move in the price of XYZ. When you wrote the put on a move in XYZ above 25 at the June expiration, you earned 14.8% on your capital as opposed to the 9.5% earned on the stock-covered call. The whopping 5.3% difference (in actual dollars, $1,146) resulted from the interest you earned on T-bills at a 6% annual rate, which was greater than one dividend collected on the stock, and from your complete avoidance of having to pay commissions to buy and to sell 1,000 shares of XYZ stock. Even if put premiums were somewhat less than the call premiums for the same expiration month and at the same strike price, they would still represent a comparatively better opportunity than writing a stock-covered call.

The successful writer of puts who does not get put earns the put premium that is lessened only by the small commission to buy T-bills and the small commission to issue the put options.

The successful writer of stock-covered calls earns the call premiums lessened by stock buy commissions, stock sell commissions, and option sell commissions.

Dear reader, how many times in your investing life have you placed an order with your broker to *buy at a limit price* a particular stock that you would like to own? Once, twice, 10 times, 20 times, 100 times, or more? And how many times did you miss getting the stock you desired, and then watch it rise in price without you being an *owner*? Once, twice, more?

It is very unsettling and disturbing to many investors to go through the analysis and research necessary to form an opinion about a stock, then to enter a limit order, thereby running the risk of stock ownership, and not profit from their judgment when the stock remains above their limit price.

Investors who write puts on stocks that they would like to own have made two decisions: (1) they *will* become owners of their desired stock at the put price *lessened* by the advance premium received; and (2) they will *not* become owners of their desired stock but be *compensated* by the winning of the put premium (less the option commission).

Writers of puts get paid for not buying the stock of their choice!

Or they get the stock of their choice at an adjusted price that is less than that at which they could have purchased the stock at the time they issued the put.

Every investor who places limit orders to buy stocks *below* where the shares are trading at the time the order is placed is essentially a put writer. He or she may not know the term or the strategy, but the investment posture of trying to acquire shares for less than the going price is identical to that of the writer of puts.

The two big differences between the investor placing buy limit orders for stocks and the writer of puts are that the put writer collects handsome sums of money for every right decision although no stock is purchased. The put writer, who has to buy stock through a put exercise, is better off (by the amount of put premium received) than the buy limit order investor who gets the order executed.

Look carefully at Tables 8.3 and 8.4, which compare put writers with stock investors who place buy limit orders below the current market price.

In Table 8.3 both investors liked XYZ stock and were willing to buy 1,000 shares at 25. Neither investor bought the stock because it remained over 25 during the life of their agreements to purchase XYZ. The put writer, however, profited handsomely from not buying XYZ.

Both investors now own 1,000 XYZ at 25 and are exposed to whatever downside risk that may occur. They are also able to participate *unrestrictedly* in any price advance of XYZ above their $25 purchase price.

The put writer adjusts the $25 cost basis in XYZ lower by the amount of the put premiums received. This places the put writer in a superior position to the buy limit order investor who also bought XYZ at 25.

Is put writing that is backed 100% by T-bills or cash equivalent reserves suitable even for conservative investors? In my opinion, the answer

Table 8.3   Put Writers and Limit Orders

In Mid-February XYZ is 26		XYZ is 30 at June Expiration (June 15)
Investor places an order to buy 1,000 XYZ @ 25 limit with the order good through June 15.		With XYZ at 30, buy limit order expires unexecuted.
Put writer issues 10 June 25 puts @ 2¹/₂.		With XYZ at 30, puts @ 25 expire unexecuted.
Collecting	$2,500	Put writer nets the $2,364 put premium.
Less full-service commission	−136	
Net proceeds	$2,364	

Table 8.4   Stock Investors and Limit Orders

In Mid-February XYZ is 26		XYZ is 20 at June Expiration	
Investor places an order to buy 1,000 XYZ @ 25 limit with the order good through June 15.		Buy limit writer has earlier purchased 1,000 shares of XYZ @ 25.	
Put writer issues 10 June 25 puts @ 2¹/₂.		Pays	$25,000
		Plus full-service commission	+453
Collecting	$2,500	Net cost	$25,453
Less full-service commission	–136		
Net proceeds	$2,364	Put writer buys 1,000 XYZ @ 25 via puts being exercised.	
		Pays	$25,000
		Plus full-service commission	+453
		Net cost	$25,453
		Less net put proceeds	–2,364
		Net proceeds	$23,089

is "yes," *if* the conservative investor completely understands the strategy *before* entering into it and *if* the investor has the emotional makeup to tolerate the fact that when a put is exercised against the writer, the writer *must pay the exercise price* even though the market price might be substantially lower.

The successful put writer whose puts go unexercised earns profits from the net put premiums and from the interest earned on the collateral backing the puts.

On those occasions when the put writer is forced to buy stock as per the agreement, three courses of action can be taken:

1. *The put writer could simply retain the stock and hope for a later price rise.* (After all, the acquired stock should have been one the investor liked at the time the put was issued.)

2. *The put writer could immediately sell the stock* that was forced on him through the put exercise. (The sell action would normally be taken if the put writer had developed a changed and negative opinion about the stock that he or she favored at the time the put was issued.)

3. *The put writer, on buying the stock via the put exercise, could immediately issue call options* now backed by stock ownership. The call option premi-

ums plus the original put premiums would provide a substantial cushion to any price drop. The call options issued might be at the same or an even lower strike price.

As the chapter nears its end, I hope that you have gained a clear insight about the various aspects of put writing that is backed by liquid cash reserves—the benefits, the risks, the alternatives of "put," and the advantages over other stock investment strategies.

What I have not touched on is the put writer's ability to relieve himself or herself of the obligation to buy stock as per the terms of the put. A put writer who undergoes a change of opinion about wanting to own stock obligated for in the "put," may rid himself or herself of the obligation through buying puts identical to those originally issued (any time before the puts are exercised).

If the purchase of the canceling-out puts is at a price higher than initially received, a loss will be sustained. If the purchase of the canceling-out puts is at a price lower than initially received, a profit will be recorded. This option marketability is primarily what has propelled listed option trading to high volume levels and has made the use of option strategy widely available to individuals as well as to institutions.

CHAPTER 9

Hire the Experts if You Are a Financial "Wreckspert!"

Many investors are attracted to covered call writing and to writing puts that are 100% backed by cash equivalents. They are attracted by the potential for greater income and by the potential for reducing stock risk.

Despite their attraction to this mode of investing and despite their understanding of the basic concepts of writing options on a conservative basis, they often do not participate in the activity to any great extent because of a variety of factors, among them the following:

- Insufficient capital to adequately diversify a portfolio.
- Lack of time to track and make investment decisions.
- Generally inadequate recordkeeping habits.
- Lack of in-depth knowledge concerning option strategies.

Many of these would-be option investors have a ready and easy solution to their desire to participate in the possible benefits of writing options. That solution is to place a portion of their assets into mutual funds that regularly engage in writing options. By investing in mutual funds that specialize in writing options, investors are hiring experts who will make the best effort to accomplish the investor's goals through use of various option strategies. These hired experts are normally available to the investor through the purchase of shares in no-load funds, load funds, and rear-end-load funds.

The funds should normally be able to do better than most individual investors because of the following:

- Having the availability of highly sophisticated computer models to help determine best values.
- Having experts who spend their full working days managing and planning the various option strategies.
- Having trading departments that can quickly execute orders to enter into and exit out of positions.
- Having large amounts of capital so that wide diversification is easily accomplished.
- Having computerized, detailed bookkeeping that makes it easier for investors to prepare tax returns.

If you do opt to invest part of your liquid assets in a mutual fund that specializes in writing options in a conservative manner, you can also obtain additional benefits. Most option-oriented mutual funds provide investors with the following:

- Guaranteed ability to sell shares at the net asset value on any business day.
- Easy dividend reinvestment.
- Convenience of one-certificate ownership.
- Automatic withdrawal programs.
- Keogh and IRA accounts and other retirement accounts.

Once you have made the decision to hire an expert in option writing to manage part of your investment portfolio, the choices available are fairly limited because only a small number of approximately 2,000 funds specialize in writing covered calls and cash-secured puts.

Of those funds that are available, most charge an initial sales charge ranging upward to 8$1/2$%. The sales charge is the investor's money that goes to benefit the salesperson and the firm but does nothing for the investor except to reduce the amount of capital placed at work in stocks, other securities, and option strategies. My suggestion for those of you who wish to place part of your assets to work in a fund employing option-writing strategy is to invest in a true no-load fund.

The annual expenses of a fund as a percentage of net assets are important but not as important as a sales charge that represents a significant portion of invested capital. The investor choosing the fund should look for the following:

- *Past performance records* over a period of several years and different market climates. Past performance is no guarantee or assurance of future performance, but it does give you some insight as to the management's capability over a particular market period.
- *Size of the fund.* A fund with only a few million dollars tends to have very high annual expenses as a percentage of net assets and to have volatile price action in its shares. Funds with $100 million and up usually can adequately compensate management personnel so as to hire and maintain quality people.

Some investors prefer to buy funds that are members of a family of funds that permit switches from one fund to another with no charge or with only a nominal charge. However, switching no-load funds presents no problems, and family fund groups are not particularly advantageous.

The choice, of course, is up to you. Guided by the preceding paragraphs, you should be able to find a home for some part of your assets in one or more of the funds that specialize in writing options contracts. These funds can be identified by the word *options* within the fund name. All these funds specialize in writing option contracts.

If you intend to invest a substantial sum of money ($25,000, $50,000, $100,000, or more) in an option writing fund, I advise that you split the sum to be invested into 12 parts and invest one part each month until the total is invested. This method is known in the financial world as dollar cost averaging, and it serves to smooth out the ups and downs of the market over a period.

You could also use dollar cost averaging over two, three, or more years, further smoothing out the ups and downs of the market. Your periodic investments buy more shares in low markets and fewer shares in high markets, thus providing for a reduction in the average cost of shares purchased.

Example

Table 9.1 shows the power of dollar cost averaging over 10 periods. The first shares bought were at 6. The last shares bought were at 6. Despite the fact that the share prices of the first and the last purchases were the same, the investing technique produces a profit because more shares are purchased when the stock is low than when the stock is high. As Table 9.1 shows, the investment of $6,000 grows to $7,050 (1,175 shares × 6 per share) with the stock unchanged from the beginning purchase price of 6.

Table 9.1   Dollar Cost Averaging

Year	Amount Invested	Price Per Share	Shares Bought
1	$ 600	6	100
2	600	5	120
3	600	4	150
4	600	3	200
5	600	4	150
6	600	5	120
7	600	6	100
8	600	10	60
9	600	8	75
10	600	6	100
	$6,000		1,175

$$\text{Average cost per share: } \frac{\$6,000}{1,175} = \$5.10$$

Dollar cost averaging is a technique that is ideally suited for mutual fund investing. In fact, many individual stock investors employ that same strategy when acquiring a large position in a favored stock.

The only really big risks in employing dollar cost averaging in a fund are that the fund can continue in a downward price trend and never recover and that the investor will lack the willpower or resources to continue the dollar cost averaging process under adverse market conditions.

WARNING

If you choose to invest in an option fund, you must understand that despite your chosen fund's past track record, staff of option experts, coterie of securities analysts, extensive computer aids, and broad diversification, your objectives of capital growth or an income level substantially higher than the yield on Treasury bills or short-term CDs *might not be met*. In fact, in adverse stock markets substantial capital erosion might occur. The opportunity afforded by funds active in options to earn high returns goes hand in hand with the possibility of capital loss. Despite this warning, however, the larger, established option writing funds could prove an excellent place for *part* of your assets that could be subjected to stock risk.

Let us quickly recap some of the things that you should look for in selecting a fund that employs option writing. They are the following:

- *Past Track Record.*   No guarantees can be extrapolated into the future as a result of examining the past. The past, however, does provide a picture of the results that management has obtained.
- *Size of Fund.*   My minimum requirement would be at least $100 million in assets.
- *Lack of a Sales Charge.*   There should be no sales charge to buy and no exit charge to sell.
- *Low Annual Expenses.*   Expenses as a percentage of net assets should be low.

The investor who is sold a particular fund by a salesperson without *an initial sales charge* should carefully ascertain the amount and conditions of any contingent deferred sales charges. Some funds that are marketed without front-end sales charges have penalties for getting out of the fund at some later date. The penalties, or exit charges, usually range from 5% to 10%, but they may be reduced to zero if the investor remains a shareholder for a stated period.

It pays to investigate before investing!

CHAPTER 10

Guide Rules for Buy Stock–Write Call Strategy

Writing call options that are backed by the necessary number of underlying shares or securities is an old strategy that has grown increasingly popular since the creation of the Chicago Board Options Exchange in 1973.

An increasing number of institutions, such as mutual funds, banks, insurance companies, and pension funds, along with hundreds of thousands of individual investors, have been won over to this investment concept.

The attraction of issuing call options against newly purchased securities is readily and easily understandable. The investment head start provided by the buyer's premium is considered to be a substantial enough edge over other stock investment strategies to provide a return greater than that provided by any of the following:

- An investment in Treasury bills.
- Common stocks that are not optioned.
- The yields on certificates of deposit.

The magnetic appeal of collecting profits in advance of a stock price move draws investors to buy stock–write call strategy like moths to a flame, despite the risk of stock ownership. The very thought of being able to legally collect hundreds or thousands of dollars of other people's money just for agreeing to give up the unknowable price potential in a common stock above a certain price for a period of time is enough to make many an investor salivate—especially since the money collected can be immediately used in partial payment for the stocks bought!

What fascinates and attracts both institutional investors and individual investors to the strategy of buy stock–write call can be readily seen from

Table 10.1, which compares potential results obtained by an owner of XYZ common stock versus those obtained by an owner of XYZ common stock who writes call options backed by the stock. The stock buyer who immediately issues calls against the just-purchased stock usually fares better than the investor who simply buys the stock in search of a profit. In fact the buy stock–write call investor fares better in three out of the four possibilities that might take place in a price move in XYZ during the life of the option.

In seeking profits from the buy stock–write call strategy, you often have three sources of profit that you can hope will provide a total return far greater than the risk-free return available from investment in Treasury bills. The profit sources are:

1. The dividends paid to you as the owner of the underlying stock.
2. The premiums you receive from option buyers.
3. Any favorable difference between the purchase price of the stock and the strike price of the call option contract.

As attractive as the buy stock–write call strategy appears on its surface, actually getting a superior return is a much more difficult task than most first-time investors realize. The task is made difficult by the number and the frequency of decisions that you must make when you employ the strategy. These decisions involve such matters as the following:

Table 10.1   Four Buy Stock–Write Call Possibilities

	Possibilities at Expiration Date of Option			
XYZ Stock Price:	1. Rises above strike price plus premium	2. Rises less than strike plus premium	3. Unchanged at end of option period	4. Declines from purchase price
Common stock owner	Fares better			
Common stock owner who writes calls		Fares better	Fares better	Fares better

- The amount of diversification in stocks for the capital available.
- Selection of stock.
- Selection of expiration date.
- Simultaneous versus delayed executions for stock and option.
- Defenses to be employed on stock price declines.

In addition to substantial decision-making, an active buy stock–write call strategist must keep meticulous records of the amount of premium received and expiration dates and must be constantly on watch for closing option purchases and rewrite opportunities.

Detractors of the buy stock–write call strategy not only decry the voluminous recordkeeping and decision-making that go with an active program but make the case that buy stock–write call strategists give up all big-winning stock positions because of calls being exercised and are left with all losing stock positions.

The buy stock–write call strategists believe that giving up an occasional big win in a stock makes sense. They figure that they:

- "Win" the entire premium from stocks that are unchanged from the purchase price at the end of the expiration period.
- "Win" the difference from stock purchase price to strike price on out-of-the-money calls issued that are exercised. That "win" is in addition to premium received.
- Can "win" a second and sometimes a third premium (or more) from rewrites on expiration of calls or buy-backs of calls.

The buy stock–write call strategists view their technique as being similar to that of the typical insurance company. Instead of insuring lives, cars, boats, or houses, these strategists assume the downside risk in stock in return for what they believe to be handsome premiums that serve to augment cash dividends received by the beneficial stock owner.

GUIDE RULES TO IMPLEMENT A
BUY–STOCK WRITE CALL PROGRAM

Users of the buy stock–write call strategy are usually decision makers who are number oriented and percentage minded. If the foregoing attributes fit you, the following nine guide rules should prove helpful should you undertake to implement buy stock–write call program.

Rule I

Diversify. Diversification has long been recognized as a technique for risk reduction for stock investors. It should also be employed by users of the buy stock–write call strategy. My recommendation is that you should invest *no more than 10%* of the capital you have committed to the buy stock–write call strategy in a particular stock. When you observe this rule, *no single stock decline* should greatly damage your portfolio assets. With substantial capital available for use in a buy stock–write call strategy, the percentage committed to any one stock should ideally be 5% or less.

Rule II

Select only quality stocks with proven dividend-paying ability. Annual dividends of 4% or more should be paid by the bulk of the stocks backing the calls you write. Those dividends plus the premium should provide for a more assured income stream.

Rule III

Select stocks that have good fundamentals. Among them are (1) a good outlook for earnings per share, (2) a price/earnings (P/E) ratio well within the range of the stock's own historic P/E ratio, (3) a good outlook for sales, and (4) the stock price in the lower or middle of its own recent price range history.

Rule IV

Write out-of-the-money calls normally. Focus on the nearest strike price above the stock purchase price. The reservation of some profit potential from the purchase price of the stock to the strike price of the call enhances the overall return on stocks that do get exercised. Retaining some of the upside profit potential in a carefully chosen stock rewards you particularly well in up markets.

Rule V

Concentrate your call writing to middle- and far-month calls. By concentrating on receiving high premiums (as compared to near-month premiums), you:

- Get more of the speculator's dollars to serve as a cushion against a stock price drop.

- Have fewer investment decisions to make when compared to near-month call writing.
- Have fewer transactions and lower commissions, and you simplify recordkeeping and the preparation of tax returns.

Rule VI

Plan capital protection strategies in advance to be employed in the event of a stock price decline. (See also Chapter 12.)

Rule VII

Set a minimum for premium acceptance. Writing call options for quarters, halves, and other small fractions is best left to the professionals in the option world who pay little or no commission and who devote their full time and efforts to the activity.

Rule VII

Deal with a discount broker or negotiate significant commission discounts on stock and option transactions with a full-service firm. Commissions play a big factor in determining the outcome of a program of buy stock–write call strategy. This action gives you the best chance for success.

Rule IX

Commit sufficient capital to the buy stock–write call strategy so that you can achieve *prudent diversification.* Trying to get diversification with small amounts of capital invariably results in a restricted choice of stocks. Usually, in the case of very limited capital, your choice has to be made among low-priced, speculative stocks that you would not normally select if you were not planning to write options. In selecting stock to back calls, place the emphasis on avoiding downside risk. Do not let an apparently high premium seduce you into owning a stock that is not your choice for a long-term investment and that does not meet your criteria for earnings, dividends, and P/E ratio. Always bear in mind that when you use the buy stock–write call strategy, you earn money on the following:

- All stocks that are higher than the purchase price at expiration of the call.
- All stocks that are equal to the purchase price at expiration of the call.

- All stocks that decline from the purchase price *less than the initial premium collected.*

The only real risks borne by the buy stock–write call strategist in an individual stock are in a stock price drop greater than the first premium collected, plus commission expenses. Losses that do occur can be somewhat lessened by additional premiums collected on new calls written after the expiration of the first call written or on new calls written after the buy-back of the first call written.

WARNING 1

Many full-service firms supply their account executives and clients with computer printouts featuring *annualized returns.* Many investors are drawn to select possibilities for high annualized returns from these computer outputs as the focus of their buy stock–write call strategy without regard to the stock fundamentals. In my view, this is the wrong way to make selections for a buy stock–write call strategy!

It is rare that high (over 25%) annualized returns are ever regularly earned on a totally *unmargined* buy stock–write call portfolio. The highest annualized returns depicted on the computer printouts usually feature low initial premiums, short periods, and far out-of-the-money calls.

Buy stocks for a buy stock–write call strategy strictly for their apparent fundamental worth based on your own research analysis or that of a respected research department or service such as Value Line. The premium collection is an important integral of a buy stock–write call strategy but must be considered *secondary* to the stock selection.

WARNING 2

Many computer models of options are available through full-service firms for purchase by individual investors. Most of the models purport to identify overvalued and undervalued options. The theory proposed by the models is for writers of calls to issue call options for those stocks deemed to be overvalued. Buyers of calls are supposed to concentrate their call purchases on those calls deemed to be undervalued by the model.

It has been my very frequent observation that a small fraction ($1/4$ to $3/8$) can change a premium's classification by the model from overvalued to undervalued and vice versa. Do not be swayed to invest in a stock just for a small fractional premium difference that might indicate that the option is overvalued.

Again, the stock holding must be your primary concern if you are a buy stock–write call strategist. In my opinion, stocks should be bought with a decidedly bullish outlook, and out-of-the-money calls should be written so that you can participate in the first part of the upmove in the stock. The total return from profit participation, premium receipts, and dividend collection should help you greatly in your search for a better return on capital committed.

The trade-off of a lower initial premium for a substantially larger profit that results from the difference in purchase price to strike price seems worthwhile to me.

CHAPTER 11

Leverage Profit Potential by Writing Calls Secured by Deep-in-the-Money Calls

By the time you have reached this chapter, I hope that you feel comfortable with certain terms of the option world that are used interchangeably and that convey the same idea—terms such as the following:

- *Writing* covered calls.
- *Selling* covered calls.
- *Issuing* covered calls.

If you do not clearly understand these terms, you should review the glossary as well as Chapter 4, "The Buy Stock–Write Call Strategy."

An option writer who issues call options and who seeks to avoid the risk of an *unlimited upside move* in the call option obligation has several ways to cover the option obligation. Under Securities and Exchange Commission (SEC) rules and Federal Reserve Board rules, call option writers are deemed to be covered as long as they maintain in their accounts approved collateral as backing for the calls issued.

Approved collateral for backing covered calls falls into the following three categories:

1. The number of shares or securities required should the call option be exercised by the holder of the call.

2. Securities (such as convertible bonds, convertible preferred shares, and warrants) that can be *immediately* and *freely* converted into the required number of shares or securities obligated for in the call issuance.

3. Long call options with the same or lower strike price and with a maturity date the same or later than the expiration date in the calls written.

In this chapter I try to help you gain insight into a covered call writing strategy used by a great number of very sophisticated and knowledgeable investors. This strategy involves substituting a deep-in-the-money long call option as collateral for a short call option issuance, instead of the shares or securities underlying the call.

Let's assume that you are attracted to shares of XYZ priced at 55. You like XYZ for its financial strength, low price/earnings (P/E) ratio, and bright earnings potential. The current annual dividend on XYZ is $1.24 per share. The current yield based on the 55 per share price is 2.25%. You could seek profits in XYZ through the following five investment strategies:

1. Buy XYZ and hope to sell XYZ at a later date for a profit.
2. Buy XYZ and immediately write at-the-market calls.
3. Buy XYZ and immediately write out-of-the-money calls.
4. Buy XYZ deep-in-the-money calls and write XYZ at-the-market calls.
5. Buy XYZ deep-in-the-money calls and write XYZ out-of-the-money calls.

Strategies 4 and 5 are the focus of this particular chapter. Carefully compare these strategies with strategies 1, 2, and 3, which involve you in direct stock ownership and the attendant downside risk.

First, let us compare the strategy of buying XYZ stock and writing an at-the-market call versus buying deep-in-the-money calls and writing at-the-market calls. Example 1 should help you understand why some investors believe collateralizing short call obligations with long deep-in-the-money calls can be less risky and potentially more rewarding than actually owning the stock to back call obligations.

Example 1

Stock XYZ is at 55, and its annual dividend is $1.24 (2.25% yield). In early February, XYZ May calls are as follows:

Strike Price	Option Price
50	7
55	5
60	3

The potentials for your buying 500 XYZ at 55 and writing 5 XYZ May 55 calls for 5 would shape up as shown in Table 11.1.

The net profit or loss would be adjusted by whatever dividends you receive as owner of the stock. The profitable return calculations are based on using the net option proceeds to apply against the amount required for the stock purchase.

All net loss or profit figures are pretax. As can be seen from Table 11.1, you as the investor bear all the downside loss potential in the stock in return for the premium. At the May expiration you could do one of the following:

- Sell the stock as per Table 11.1.
- Hold the stock if it is below the exercise price, and hope for a price recovery.
- Hold the stock if it is below the exercise price, and write new calls.

Your potential, if you were to buy 5 XYZ in-the-money May 50 calls at 7 and write 5 May 55 calls for 5, would be as shown in Table 11.2.

Table 11.1   Possible Outcomes of Stock Purchase at the Market[a]

XYZ Possible Prices	Stock Cost Plus Buy Commission	Call Option Proceeds Less Sell Commission	At Expiration, Net Profit (Loss) if Stock Sold[b]	
35	$27,925	$2,400	($8,345)	(29.8 %)
45	27,925	2,400	(3,405)	(12.19%)
55	27,925	2,400	1,975	7.7%
65	27,925	2,400	1,975	7.7%
75	27,925	2,400	1,975	7.7%

[a]Call write strategy at May expiration with commissions at full-service rates. Commission costs could be reduced if the investor negotiated a discount through the full-service firm or dealt with a discount firm.
[b]Stock sale commissions included.

Table 11.2   Possible Outcomes of Deep-in-the-Money Call Purchase[a]

XYZ Possible Prices at May Expiration	Deep-in-the-Money Call Purchase, Includes Buy Commission	Sold 5 XYZ May 55 @ 5 Option Proceeds Less Sell Commission	At Expiration, Net Profit (Loss) Option Sale and Purchase, Commissions Included	
35	$3,610	$2,400	($1,210)	
45	3,610	2,400	(1,210)	
55	3,610	2,400	1,190	98.3%
65	3,610	2,400	1,008	83.3%
75	3,610	2,400	885	73.1%

[a]Call purchase, at-the-market call write strategy at May expiration. Commissions at full-service rates.

In Table 11.2 the assumption is made that at expiration any *long* in-the-money calls with intrinsic value will be sold for the intrinsic value *less* the commission. Any *short* in-the-money calls will be purchased for the intrinsic value *plus* the commission.

Notice that no matter how far below 50 XYZ drops, you can lose no more than the $1,210 outlay over the proceeds of the premium initially received from the calls sold. That risk reduction compares very favorably against the risk assumed by investors owning the stock, as shown in Table 11.1.

When examining the positive results, you should notice the percentage return on the capital at risk. The percentage return for the investor who collateralizes with a deep-in-the-money call is far greater than for the investor who collateralizes with the stock.

In Table 11.1 the investor employed $25,525 of capital (stock cost $27,925 less net option premium of $2,400). In Table 11.2 the investor employed $1,210 of capital (option purchase cost $4,115 less net option sale proceeds of $2,400). The investor in Table 11.2 could derive money market income on $24,315 not placed at risk. The money market earnings could normally far outweigh any dividend received by the stock owner in Table 11.1. Those extra money market fund dollars would augment any net premium dollars earned from the call writing activity to produce a net return on a comparable amount of capital.

Notice carefully that the example of XYZ May 50 calls at 7 with the stock at 55 represents a 2-point premium over the intrinsic worth of 5 (55 – 5). That is a very high premium! Very frequently investors will find deep-in-the-money call options available to purchase with little ($1/4$ to $1/2$) time premium. When those opportunities are available, they make outstanding collateral for writing calls. Writing out-of-the-money calls that are backed by deep-in-the-money calls offers exceptional reward potential should the stock at expiration be at the out-of-the-money call strike price or higher.

Let's examine Example 2 carefully. It compares writing out-of-the-money calls backed by stock with writing out-of-the-money calls backed by deep-in-the-money calls.

Example 2

As in Example 1, XYZ is at 55. XYZ annual dividend is $1.24 (2.25% yield). In early February, XYZ May calls are as follows:

Strike Price	Option Price
50	7
55	5
60	3

The potential return for an investor buying 500 XYZ at 55 and writing XYZ May 60 calls at 3 would be as shown in Table 11.3.

The net profit or loss would be adjusted by any dividends received as an XYZ stockowner. The profitable return calculations are based on using

Table 11.3   Possible Outcomes of Stock Purchase Out of the Money[a]

XYZ Possible Prices	Stock Cost Plus Commission	Proceeds Less Sell Commission	Net Profit (Loss) if Stock Sold[b]	
35	$27,925	$1,417	($9,328)	(33.4%)
45	27,925	1,417	(4,388)	(15.7%)
55	27,925	1,417	567	2.1%
60	27,925	1,417	3,047	11.4%
65	27,925	1,417	3,047	11.4%

[a]Call write strategy at May expiration. Commission at full-service rates. Commission costs could be reduced by negotiating a discount or by using a discount broker.
[b]Stock sale commissions included.

the net option proceeds to apply against the amount required for the stock purchase. All net profit and loss figures are *pretax*.

As can be seen from Table 11.3, the investor who buys XYZ stock to collateralize out-of-the-money calls bears all the downside risk potential in the stock in return for the premium collected for issuing the out-of-the-money call options.

At the May expiration date, the investor could do one of the following:

- Sell XYZ stock as per Table 11.3.
- Hold XYZ stock if it is below the 60 exercise price, and hope for an upward price move.
- Hold XYZ stock if it is below the 60 exercise price and write new calls at the same strike or a different strike.

Notice that no matter how high XYZ might be above 60 at expiration, the profit remains the same. This is because the stock was exercised and sold at the exercise price of 60, adjusted by all commissions at the full service rate.

In Table 11.4 the assumption is made that at expiration any long in-the-money calls with intrinsic value will be sold for the intrinsic value less the commission. Any short in-the-money calls will be purchased for the intrinsic value plus the commission.

Again, notice that no matter how far XYZ shares decline, the investor can never lose more than $2,193, which represents the net outlay for the call options purchased less the net money received from call options sold. This reduction in risk compares very favorably against the risk assumed by investors owning the stock, as in Table 11. 3.

In examining the positive results, you should notice the percentage return on the capital at risk. The percentage return for the investor who collateralizes with a deep-in-the-money call is far greater than for the investor who collateralizes with the stock.

In Table 11.3, the investor employed $26,508 ($27,925 stock purchase cost less $1,417 from net call option proceeds).

The investor in Table 11.4 could also derive money market income on the $25,732 not placed at risk. The money market earnings would normally far outweigh any dividends collected by the stockowner in Table 11.3.

Those dollars earned in a money market fund would augment any net premium dollars earned from writing the out-of-the-money calls backed by the in-the-money calls. That total net return should be compared with the capital employed and the return earned by the out-of-the-money call

Table 11.4   Possible Outcomes of Deep-in-the-Money Call
Purchase, Out-of-the-Money Call Write[a]

XYZ Possible Prices at May Expiration	Purchased 5 XTZ May 50 Deep-in-the-Money @ 7, Buy Commission Included	Sold 5 XYZ May 60 Out-of-the-Money Calls @ 3, Less Sell Commission	At Expiration, Net Profit (Loss) Option Sale and Purchase, Commissions Included	
35	$3,610	$1,417	($2,193)	
45	3,610	1,417	(2,193)	
55	3,610	1,417	307	13.9%
60	3,610	1,417	2,680	122%
65	3,610	1,417	2,552	116%

[a]At May expiration. Commissions at full-service rates.

writer who collateralizes with stock. The deep-in-the-money call used as collateral offers call writers the following advantages:

- Substantial downside risk reduction compared with the risk of stock ownership.
- Total profit potential from premiums and money market funds (interest earned on money not used to buy stock), which approximates (and is sometimes greater than) that of stock that is collateralized.

CHAPTER 12

Defensive Strategies for Short Call Option Positions Secured by Stock

Writers of covered calls who use the ownership of the underlying shares of securities as collateral must bear the risk of a drop in the stock price. A fall in value might be significantly greater than the initial premium received. The informed and forward-thinking writer of covered calls should become familiar with the various possible courses of action to take in the event of a severe price drop in securities used as collateral.

Example

Let's assume that in early October you buy 500 XYZ at 33 and issue 5 April 35 calls for 3.

The advance premium of $1,500 less commissions offers an apparently nice cushion against a possible drop in the value of XYZ shares. You hope that the calls in April will be exercised and that the stock will be sold at 35, thus providing another 2 points of profit reduced by the attendant stock commissions. Any dividends due serve to augment the overall hoped-for return. With those assumptions in mind, let's examine the following scenario.

In early January, XYZ has declined from 33 to 29. The April 35 call, originally issued for 3, has fallen to $1/2$ because of the following:

- *The passage of time.* Call options are a *wasting asset*—the value of the options decreases as the time to expiration grows shorter. Out-of-the-money options normally waste at a more rapid rate. although the waste factor is detrimental to the option holder, it is beneficial to the option writer.

- *The decline in value* of XYZ shares from 33 to 29.

This chapter turns the spotlight on the *four defensive tactics* available to the writer of stock-covered calls who experiences a severe price erosion in the shares underlying the short call obligation.

Defense I

You could and should reevaluate XYZ at the now lower level of 29. Make your reevaluation on the basis of current information about XYZ's earning prospects, dividend maintenance or dividend increase prospects, and a comparison of XYZ's price/earnings (P/E) ratio with XYZ's own past historical record. This information is readily available from Standard & Poor's (S&P), Value Line, and other analytical services. Furthermore, if you are doing business with a full-service firm, get that firm's current report and opinion about the outlook for XYZ.

Also consider the general market action if you are holding XYZ at a loss. Is the entire market down in proportion to the drop in XYZ? Is the market stable, or up, and XYZ down?

Those are just some of the questions you must resolve before committing to one of the four possible defensive actions.

Defense I involves your making a value judgment about XYZ and concluding that there is nothing really adverse in the current or future outlook for XYZ's fundamentals.

With that conclusion made, you could simply decide to remain long XYZ at its depressed price. If at the end of the April expiration, XYZ is still below 35, you can issue another call and collect more premium dollars to further reduce the risk of stock decline. This might be considered a do-nothing strategy. However, you have done something! You have reevaluated XYZ and your short call position and have decided to maintain both positions.

Defense II

After reviewing the fundamentals of XYZ and getting research information (S&P or Value Line) and opinions from a full-service firm's research department (when possible), you may conclude that XYZ is no longer attractive and that it may continue to fall below the current 29 price. Having arrived at that conclusion, you may opt for Defense II.

You are now negative on XYZ and its prospects, and you are afraid of an even sharper decline in its price. Using Defense II, you enter two simultaneous orders:

1. Sell the 500 XYZ shares at the market.
2. Buy 5 XYZ calls at the market identical to the ones you initially sold (April 35s). The call purchase automatically cancels out the obligation you originally incurred.

If you sell the shares at 29, you will suffer a 4-point loss on the 500 shares. The loss will equal $2,000 (5 × $400) plus the commission expenses of buying and selling XYZ.

If you buy the XYZ calls at $1/2$, as in our illustration, you will gain $1,250 less commission expenses. Table 12.1 makes clear the results of the stock sale at a loss and the option purchase at a profit. After executing the stock sale and the call purchase, you are again in a cash position, having sustained a relatively small loss on a stock that lost favor in the market and in your eyes.

Now returned to a cash position, you can select another stock (using your own established criteria) and immediately issue a covered call in the hope that the premium you will immediately receive from issuing the new call will restore all the dollars you lost in the XYZ adventure and provide some additional cash beyond what was lost.

Defense III

In this defense, as a writer of a covered call, you have carefully reviewed XYZ's fundamental outlook and have concluded that XYZ shares appear to have little additional downside price risk and that there are some prospects for price recovery over the near term and intermediate term.

Table 12.1 Stock Sale–Option Purchase

Bought 500 XYZ @ 33	$16,500	Sold 5 XYZ April 35 calls @ 3	$1,500
Sold 500 XYZ @ 29	–14,500	Bought 5 XYZ April 35	
Loss	(2,000)	calls @ $1/2$	–250
Full-service commissions to		Profit	1,250
buy and sell stock	+585	Full-service commissions	
Net loss on stock trades	$ 2,585	to buy and sell calls	-122
		Net profit on call option trades	$1,128

Stock net loss[a]	($2,585)
Call option net profit	–1,128
Combined net loss	($1,457)

[a]Any dividends received would cushion the loss.

You decide to retain your ownership XYZ, making the decision on the basis of your analysis of the currently available information. You peruse the option price tables for XYZ call options. In January, XYZ calls are quoted as follows:

Strike Price	April	July
30	2	3^1/$_2$
35	^{1}/$_2$	1^1/$_2$

In addition to making the decision to retain XYZ stock, you employ Defense III and decide to collect additional premium to further cushion a possible price decline. The way to collect additional premium above the earlier October receipt is to do the following:

- Buy 5 XYZ April 35s at ^{1}/$_2$, thereby completely eliminating the April 35 call option obligation.
- Issue new calls for more than the ^{1}/$_2$ paid to relieve the outstanding obligation.

With the purchase of 5 XYZ April 35 calls eliminating the original obligation, you now have two ways to collect additional premium income to further protect your stock ownership of 500 XYZ:

1.   You can write 5 July 35s for 1^1/$_2$. This produces $750 (1^1/$_2$ × 5) of new premium income (less the option commissions) to cushion any possible further price erosion in XYZ. It also lets you participate in a possible price recovery on XYZ to the 35 level.

2.   You can write 5 July 30s for 3^1/$_2$. This produces $1,750 (3^1/$_2$ × 5) less the option commission. Although this provides a substantial cushion against a further price drop in XYZ, it locks you into selling XYZ at 30 if the option is exercised.

As shown in Table 12.2, by collecting a second premium you accomplish the following:

- You *increase* your downside protection for your holding of 500 XYZ shares.
- You *retain* the exercise price of 35 and the price recovery possibility in XYZ from the $29 level.
- You *extend* the period of the call obligation from April to July.

Table 12.2 Results of Second Premium

In October XYZ is 33		In January XYZ is 29	
Buy 500 XYZ @ 33	$16,500		
Full-service buy commission	+305		
Net cost	$16,805		
Sell 5 XYZ April 35s @ 3	$ 1,500	Buy 5 XYZ April 35s @ 1/2	$250
Full-service sell commission	–83	Full-service buy commission	+39
Net premium received	$ 1,417	Net cost	$289
		$1,128 Net profit on option trades	
		Sell 5 XYZ July 35s @ 1 1/2	$750
		Full-service sell commission	–70
		Net premium receipt	$680
Total net premiums	($1,417 + $680) – $2,097		

The action of taking a second premium would normally be undertaken by a writer who retained a more bullish outlook toward XYZ shares.

In the language of the option world, this action would be called a *rollout*, a term that signifies that the writer has done the following:

- Extended (rolled out) the period in the call obligation.
- Maintained the same strike in the new call as in the old call that was "extinguished" through an offsetting purchase.

Table 12.3 depicts your position if you opted to buy in your existing call obligation (April 35s) and issue new calls at a lower strike price and with a different and longer expiration period.

If you are called at 30 by the July expiration, you do the following:

Sell 500 XYZ @ 30	$15,000
Full-service sell commission	–287
Net premium receipt	$14,713

Your net loss on stock transactions is $2,092, and your net gain from the two options is $2,791. Your total net is $699 on the combined and completed stock and option transaction.

As shown in Table 12.3, you were able to extricate yourself from what you perceived as a losing situation (stock decline from 33 to 29) by rolling

Table 12.3   Buy Old Call, Issue New Calls

In October XYZ is 33		In January XYZ is 29	
Buy 500 XYZ @ 33	$16,500		
Full-service buy commission	+305		
Net cost	$16,805		
		Buy 5 XYZ April 35s @ 1/2	$250
Sell 5 XYZ April 35s @ 3	$ 1,500	Full-service buy commission	+39
Full-service sell commission	−83	Net cost	$289
Net premium receipt	$ 1,417		

Net profit on option trades ($1,417 − $289) = $1,128

		Sell 5 XYZ July 30s @ 3 1/2	$1,750
		Full-service sell commission	−87
		Net premium receipt	$1,663

out to a more distant expiration month and rolling out to a lower striking price than that in the first issued calls.

If you had been called at the new lower strike price of 30, you would still have wound up with a profit as a result of the two premiums you collected. That profit is net of all commission expenses and augmented by any cash dividends received!

No wonder so many number-oriented investors are attracted to stock-covered call writing! A loss on a stock position can result in an overall net profit after calculating in option profits! Wow!

Easy? No! Simple? No! Viable? Yes! Stock-covered call writing accompanied by the knowledge and use of defensive strategies can help conservative investors in their constant search for higher returns.

Defense IV

The fourth of the defensive actions you can take as a writer of stock-covered calls with a stock that has declined (as per our example) from 33 to 29 is to purchase calls identical to the ones you originally sold, thereby canceling out the short call obligation. You retain ownership of XYZ shares on the basis of your careful review and analysis of XYZ's fundamental outlook for sale, earnings, and dividends.

The January purchase of 5 XYZ April 35s at 1/2 versus the original sale in October of 5 XYZ April 35s at 3 produces a net profit of $1,128 after all commission expenses.

You retain the 500 XYZ shares unoptioned, hoping for a price rise in

XYZ that would enable you to sell the same April 35 calls again at a price substantially higher than the purchase at $1/2$ or perhaps to obtain a very high premium for the July 35s.

You reap the bulk of the benefit from the price decline in the original April 35s and are bullish enough about XYZ's prospects not to want to issue strike price calls lower than 35 or to sell more distant 35 calls for a low price.

The reader should understand that there is no one defensive strategy to employ (on a stock price decline) that is always correct.

The investor in a declining stock subject to a short call obligation is always faced with:

- Developing opinions about the stock's future prospects from the now lower price level.

- Selecting a defensive strategy to employ to protect the capital invested in the stock.

Remember: Being a conservative investor means being an informed investor!

CHAPTER 13

Buying Calls Can Make Sense Even for Conservative Investors

Buying call options is normally viewed as a highly speculative option activity, one that is somewhat akin to gambling. In fact, most market observers and participants equate option buying with betting on horse races, betting on dog races, buying instant lottery tickets, and casino gambling. In some respects, buying call options (or puts) *is* like gambling, particularly in the sense that it is a positively skewed investment activity. *Positively skewed* is a mathematical term used to indicate that the amount placed at total risk of loss is finite, or fixed, and that the amount that could be won is much larger than the amount that could be lost.

Although buying call or put options is often placed in the gambling category, it differs greatly from normal forms of gambling in that all losses from buying options qualify as tax deductible items! Any losses from buying options can be used to offset capital gains earned! In addition, any losses from buying options that are not used to offset capital gains may be used as deductions against highest taxed income up to $3,000 in any single tax year.

Losses from buying options that are greater than those used to offset capital gains and as a deduction against highest taxed income may be carried forward indefinitely into future years until they are used up as deductions or offsets to capital gains earned. The Internal Revenue Service obviously views option speculation as being very different from the common, well-known forms of gambling.

In addition to tax benefits, losing option purchasers usually get more time to root for a winner! In a horse or a dog race, the result is known in a couple of minutes. In casino gambling, the outcome is determined in seconds. Through option purchases, the investor (gambler!) often has months to cheer for a winner.

A third benefit of option purchases over other forms of gambling is the right option purchasers have to change their minds and terminate the investment. You can buy a put or a call with a life of six months, but you can change your mind and terminate the position after holding it a few days or weeks. The sum realized from the termination may be more or less than the sum originally invested, or bet. But at least some recovery is possible if you change your opinion.

Once you have placed a bet on a race and the race has begun, can you make a change? No! When the roulette wheel spins, can you make a change? No! By now you should have grasped that buying options, although it can be and most often is a speculative activity, is certainly not analogous to gambling. In fact, there are several activities in purchasing options that even conservative investors should understand and possibly employ when the proper occasion arises.

Let's examine several examples of situations in which conservatives might buy call options and still be considered to be in a conservative investment posture.

Example 1

Substituting a deep-in-the-money long call option (with little time premium) for common stock in order to collateralize a short call option.

Let's assume that XYZ is a volatile stock that you have been closely watching. Judging the outlook to be positive for near-term earnings growth and for a dividend increase, you decide to write covered calls. In late February with XYZ at 44, the call option quotations for the June expiration are as follows:

Strike Price	Option Price
35	10
40	5
45	3
47½	2

You could simply buy 500 XYZ (the position being considered an amount appropriate for your overall stock risk exposure) and write 5 XYZ June 47½s for 2. Instead of that "normal" form of a covered write, you decide to substitute a long deep-in-the-money call as collateral for the June 47 1/2s issued instead of buying XYZ stock.

By substituting 5 long June 40 calls at 5 for 500 XYZ shares at 44, you accomplish the following:

- You reduce your out-of-pocket cash to $1,500, plus the commission expense [(5 × $500) – (5 × $200)].
- You reduce risk in the event that your judgment of XYZ is wrong and it plummets to below 40 and remains under 40 at expiration. Your maximum possible loss is $1,500 plus commission. That loss would be softened by interest earnings on the amount *not used* to buy 500 XYZ at 44.
- You avoid commission expenses should XYZ June 47 1/2s expire worthless.
- On a substantial price rise in XYZ above 47 1/2, you can sell the long June 40 calls for their intrinsic worth (or intrinsic worth plus possibly a small time premium) while simultaneously buying 5 June 47 1/2s for their intrinsic worth (plus some small time premium) to cancel out the short call obligation.
- Upon liquidation of both the long June 40s and the short June 47 1/2s at intrinsic value, you realize $3,750 (5 × $750) less commissions and less the original out-of-pocket option cost of $1,500.

Example 2

Cashing in stock profits and retaining a future interest in a stock rise.

Many an investor has been perceptive enough to purchase a chosen stock at a low price and then have it rise to lofty levels. Upon seeing the stock reach the high level, the fortunate investor is often faced with questions as to what action to take with the profitable shareholdings, such as the following:

- Should the stock be sold and profit collected?
- Should part of the stock holding be sold and the rest retained for possible further price appreciation?
- Should the stock continue to be held, incurring the risk of a price collapse back to the original purchase-price level or even lower?
- Should call options be written limiting further gain to a specific amount but retaining risk of a big fall in price?
- Should stop loss orders be entered (where permitted by the exchange) at some point below the current price of the shares?

There may not be an overall perfect answer to each of these questions, but for many investors a viable course would be to take the two following steps:

1.   Sell all the shares and cash in on a wonderful profit! That action not only makes the investor feel good, but it completely eliminates the possibility of a price fall that could eradicate all or most of the hard-won profit (or even create a loss!).

2.   With a small percentage of the profits (5% to 10%), buy call options on the stock sold so that a future interest in a further price rise is kept.

If you are in this situation and take these two steps, you will be left with your original capital. You would also have 90% to 95% of your profit out of the stock and available to reinvest in other stocks, to secure fixed income, or to put to any other use you desire.

Two of the most disheartening experiences for an investor in stock are (1) to let a larger profit evaporate or turn into a loss, and (2) to sell a stock and then watch it rise substantially within a short time after the sale. Both of these upsetting experiences can be avoided if you are knowledgeable about options by purchasing calls on stocks that you sell at large profits. This is true as long as your allocation of funds to buy calls represents only a small fraction of the profits you have earned.

As for the calls you choose to buy to retain a future interest in a price rise, my vote is to purchase in-the-money calls, which tend to move quickly and reflect any upward price action in the underlying shares. In my opinion, the expiration date of the calls you purchase should have a minimum life of three months. See Table 13.1, where these principles are illustrated.

In the situation illustrated by Table 13.1:

- You cash in a net profit of $19,330.
- You risk $2,090 on the call purchase hoping to participate in a possible further rise in XYZ, limiting risk to the amount used to buy the call.
- You have $27,465 available for reinvestment.

Example 3

Possible courses of action to take if you have experienced a sharp price decline in a stock purchase.

If the price of a stock that you are holding drops sharply, if you are

Table 13.1   Buying In-the-Money Calls

In January		In June XYZ is 60	
You buy 500 XYZ @ 20	$10,000	You sell 500 XYZ @ 60	$30,000
Plus full-service commission	+225	Less full-service commission	–445
Net cost of stock	$10,225	Net proceeds	$29,555
		You buy 5 October 57½	
		calls @ 4	$ 2,000
		Plus full-service commission	+90
		Net cost of calls	$ 2,090
		Net proceeds of stock sale	$29,555
		Net cost of calls	–2,090
		Net proceeds available	$27,465

prudent and conservative, you should reanalyze the rationale that influenced you to buy shares at a price much higher than the current level. Get up-to-date information from Standard & Poor's, Value Line, and any other analytical source that is available to try to arrive at a decision on which of the three following courses of action you should take.

1. Buy more shares at the now lower price to average down. A new purchase at a lower price produces an average share cost that is less than the cost of the shares you first bought. The *averaging down* makes it possible to get to a breakeven point below the price at which you originally purchased the stock.
2. Sell the shares and accept the loss.
3. Hold the shares and hope for a recovery to or above your original purchase price.

Let's suppose that you had bought 500 XYZ shares at 44. After the purchase, XYZ declined in value to 34. You properly reanalyze XYZ and conclude that XYZ represents an even more excellent value at the 34 level than at the original purchase price of 44. The outlook for positive sales and earnings growth appears to be superior. The price/earnings (P/E) ratio is lower than its historical past and lower than the market multiple (the P/E ratio of the general market).

Fortified by your reinvestigation, you decide to take the *first* course of action—increase your stake in XYZ. There are two methods available to increase your participation in XYZ.

1. You could buy 500 more shares at the 34 price, reducing your average cost to 39.

2. You could buy 5 calls on XYZ at 30. With the stock at 34, deep-in-the-money calls should be available at a small time premium.

Let's take a look at the risk and reward potential in each of the two methods (see Tables 13.2 and 13.3).

In the situation illustrated by Table 13.2:

1. You have invested $39,687 in the two stock purchases ($22,375 + $17,312).

2. Your average cost per share is $39.68 including commission.

3. You bear all the risk of a further price decline in 1,000 XYZ.

4. You have unlimited profit potential in a price rise above $39.68 per share for the 1,000 XYZ shares you hold.

In the situation illustrated by Table 13.3:

1. You have invested $24,720 in the stock purchase and call purchase ($22,375 + $2,345).

Table 13.2   Averaging Down by Stock Purchase

In January XYZ is 44		In July XYZ is 34	
You buy 500 XYZ @ 44	$22,000	You buy 500 XYZ @ 34	$17,000
Plus full-service commission	+375	Plus full-service commission	+312
Net cost	$22,375	Net cost	$17,312

Table 13.3   Averaging Down by In-the-Money Call Purchase

In early July XYZ October 30 calls are quoted:

Strike Price 30 In January XYZ is 44		Option Price 4 1/2 In July XYZ is 34	
You buy 500 XYZ @ 44	$22,000	You buy 5 XYZ Oct 30s @ 4 1/2	$2,250
Plus full-service commission	+375	Plus full-service commission	+95
Net cost of stock	$22,375	Net cost of calls	$2,345

2. If XYZ is 40 by the October expiration, you could cash out both the stock and the option positions and be approximately even, including all commission costs in and out.

3. Upon a severe price drop in XYZ below 30 by the October expiration, you lose the entire call premium and suffer the additional loss in value of the 500 XYZ originally bought at 44.

4. You have unlimited profit potential above XYZ (through the October expiration) for the 1,000 XYZ shares controlled (500 controlled by the call option right to buy XYZ at 30 and 500 controlled by direct ownership through purchase at 44).

Comparing Tables 13.2 and 13.3, you should notice that the averaging down through the purchase of in-the-money calls with little time premium (Table 13.3) is a superior strategy (in my opinion) to averaging down with a share purchase that is equal in number to the original purchase (Table 13.2). There are three reasons why averaging down with an in-the-money call purchase is a better course of action than acquiring an equal number of shares at the now lower market price:

1. It takes less out-of-pocket capital to buy in-the-money calls than it does to acquire the equivalent shares.

2. The risk of loss because of another sharp price decline in XYZ is less in the call-purchase-averaging-down example than in the stock-purchase-averaging-down example.

3. The $14,967 ($39,687 – $24,720) not used to buy additional shares can earn interest in a money fund.

You may be perceptive enough to see that if you average down through the purchase of an additional equivalent number of shares, you could continue to hold the shares indefinitely in hope of a price recovery in XYZ.

Let's play the "what if" game for a moment. What if at the October expiration XYZ were $20? $25? $30? At 20, you could buy 500 XYZ from your money fund reserve of $14,967, plus the interest earnings, and still be nearly $5,000 better off than if you had averaged down at 34 with a purchase of 500 more XYZ shares—and that is after recording a total loss of $2,345 in the expiration of 5 XYZ October 30 calls.

At 25, you could buy 500 XYZ from your money fund reserve of $14,967, plus interest earnings, and still be nearly $2,500 better off than if you had averaged down at 34 with a purchase of 500 more XYZ shares— and that also would be after recording a loss of $2,345 at the expiration of 5 XYZ October 30 calls.

At 30, you could buy 500 XYZ from your money fund reserve of $14,967, plus interest earnings, and still be little or no worse off than if you had averaged down in July at 34 with a purchase of 500 more XYZ shares. The recorded loss of $2,345 from the expired October 30 calls would be a deductible item for that tax year even though you continued to hold XYZ into the following year.

CHAPTER 14

Strategies for Investors with Long Profitable Option Positions

Many investors, even so-called conservative investors, are often attracted to the outright purchase of puts and calls because of a belief in the potential for large profits over a relatively short period. In addition to being drawn to the large profit potential that they believe exists in a particular stock, they are attracted to option purchases because of the following:

- The risk is finite and exactly limited to the amount paid for the option.
- The leverage is large because a relatively small amount of option dollars can control a significantly larger number of dollars in underlying shares.

Truly conservative investors who wish to follow their judgment of a stock's profit potential by committing to an option purchase should use only those funds that are a tiny fraction of their liquid assets. The sum invested in the purchase of options should also be one the total loss of which would not be either emotionally upsetting or financially destructive in any significant way.

Some conservative investors regularly allocate part of the capital gains they earn from other investments to the purchase of stock options. They theorize that if an option purchase results in a partial or total loss, the gain previously recorded is simply reduced, or offset, by the amount of the loss. This attitude provides for a less pressured and less emotional outlook when they speculate in stock options.

WINNING CALL STRATEGIES

Once you have made the decision to purchase stock options, you should preplan courses of action to take should the option purchase turn into a winning situation. This preplan should particularly focus on the action that you will take if the option becomes very profitable early in its life.

Let's first examine the possibilities for the purchaser of call options. Assume that in early January you buy 10 XYZ July 20 call options at 3 each. In early February, XYZ rises to 26. The July 20s are trading at $6^1/2$. Other call option quotations on XYZ are the following:

Strike Price	April Option Price	July Option Price
20	$6^1/4$	$6^1/2$
25	$2^1/4$	$3^1/4$
30	$3/4$	$1^1/4$

Winning Call Option Strategy I

Sell half of the winning position. When an option purchase has doubled in value early in the life of the option, sell enough of the options held (assuming that more than one was purchased) to allow you to recover approximately all the capital you originally used to purchase the option. No matter what happens to the option price after the sale of half of the contracts that doubled in value, you will not be exposed to the loss of any significant portion of the capital that you committed to the option purchase.

Options are very volatile investment instruments, and they have a relatively short and wasting life. The sale of half of a position that has doubled in value not only leaves your original capital intact, but it provides you with an ongoing option investment that could do one of the following:

- Continue to appreciate significantly.
- Remain approximately the same.
- Decline to zero worth at expiration.

At the expiration, you can sell the remaining contracts, if they are above the call option strike price, for their intrinsic value, which would be an additional profit for you.

Some experienced option purchasers do not wait for an exact double in value of an options purchase before retrieving their entire initial capital. Understanding the vagaries of both the stock and the option markets, experienced option purchasers tend to hedge their bets rather quickly by selling enough of their purchased contracts to allow complete recovery of capital. They keep the rest of the options for "free" and for whatever additional rewards that might occur. Should the retained options again substantially increase in value, part of the remaining position could be sold to guarantee an overall profit while still maintaining a leveraged interest in a continued rise.

Winning Call Strategy II

Sell higher strike price calls backed by lower strike price calls owned.   Another way for you to win on your purchase of 10 XYZ July 20s in early January at 3 and your experience of the rise in option value to 6¹/₂ would be to write calls collateralized by the calls you own. In early February, you review the call option quotations for XYZ, which are as follows:

Strike Price	April Call Option Price	July Call Option Price
20	6¹/₄	6¹/₂
25	2¹/₄	3¹/₄
30	³/₄	1¹/₄

You could decide to write 10 XYZ July 25s for 3¹/₄ that are completely covered by the ownership of 10 XYZ July 20s. (A long lower strike call is approved collateral for a short higher strike call on the same stock, as long as the expiration month in the short call is the same or less distant than in the long call.) On the sale of 10 July 25s at 3¹/₄, you recoup approximately the amount invested in the purchase of 10 July 20s, including commission costs. You are then in a "could win but not lose" situation, a situation that any investor would love.

If at the July expiration XYZ were *20 or under,* both the long 20s and the short 25s expire worthless. You break even on your entire investment.

If at the July expiration XYZ were *over 20 or under 25,* the long 20s would be sold for the intrinsic value, which would represent profit to the investor (maximum $5,000 less option commission). The short 25s could expire worthless.

If at the July expiration XYZ were *over 25*, the long 20s would be sold for intrinsic value. The short 25s would be bought for intrinsic value. You would realize $5,000, less the options commissions.

In this example there are many possible variations of writing short calls backed by long calls. You could have chosen to write April 25s or July 30s, each choice varying the possibility for risk and reward. You must make a judgment at the time that is based on your opinion about the underlying stock and the market. Regardless of your choice, though, it seems prudent to me to partially or fully hedge a winning long option position so as to lock in profit or restrict loss.

Winning Call Option Strategy III

Sell all of the winning position. Once you have committed risk capital to the purchase of options on a chosen stock and have experienced an approximate doubling in the option's value, as in the foregoing example, you may decide to cash in. In the example, the option value of the July 20s rose from 3 in early January to 6½ by early February.

Despite the fact that the option had approximately five months of life to expiration, you could simply decide to sell the entire position and regain your initial capital as well as a handsome profit. Nothing wrong with that! You could base your decision on your judgment that the price rise has been very rapid and could possibly recede as quickly as it has risen.

Once cashed out with a fine profit earned, you could continue to observe XYZ. You might hope for and wait for an opportunity to buy the July 25s at 3 or even less again. Many investors have traded in and out of the same option contract successfully several times during the option's life.

Again, these are judgments that must be made by the individual investor at the time, on the basis of the investor's evaluation of the stock and of the market at the time.

There is no single *right* strategy that should always be employed when you are dealing with a winning option holding. Some method of profit taking or risk reduction does seem to be the most prudent course to follow to prevent a winning situation from completely escaping and possibly becoming a loss situation.

Winning Call Option Strategy IV

Retain the entire position. Some very intelligent purchasers of call options have a different view regarding dealing with a winning option position early in the life of their selected option. Their viewpoint is to try to maximize profits that result from a well-thought-out and well-researched opinion about a common stock. They believe in letting profits run. Once they have a winning position, they dislike cutting its rather unlimited potential by employing any of the previously three strategies discussed:

I.   Selling half of the position, which limits future profits to the half retained.

II. Writing calls against calls owned, thereby absolutely limiting profit to a predetermined amount.

III. Selling the entire position, thus ending further profit from a continued price rise.

These particular option purchasers seek the really big win of 5, 10, 20, or more times their original investment! They have the mental toughness to accept the possibility that the profit in hand could eventually be eliminated and turned into a loss. It is easier for them to accept the possibility of the profit becoming a loss than to place limits of any kind on their winning position. They also believe that their chances for the really big gain are greater by simply maintaining a position than by trading successfully in and out of an option during its life.

After observing and participating in the option market for more than 20 years, I have formed some very definite conclusions as to what actions should be taken by an option buyer experiencing a substantial rise in option holdings early in the life of the option. It is probably obvious that I believe most purchasers of options will do better employing some kind of hedging strategy with winning option positions instead of simply holding on and going for broke. My preferences lean toward Strategy I.

WINNING PUT STRATEGIES

You may have noticed that the foregoing has been addressed to the problem of what to do with winning call positions. You may be wondering if winning put strategies differ from those that might be employed in winning call situations.

Winning Put Strategies I, III, and IV

Dealing with winning long put holdings is slightly different from dealing with winning long call option holdings. One big difference is that profits from long call options are essentially unlimited. There is no finite limit to the amount that you can earn.

With long put holdings, the profit is always limited—from the strike price down to zero less the cost of the puts. Because zero is highly unlikely, the profit potential of the long put is further limited to some price above zero.

With those caveats in mind, strategies to employ with winning put holdings are the same as those given for winning option Strategies I, III, and IV. The only strategy for puts that differs from those for calls is Strategy II.

Winning Put Strategy II

Write lower strike price puts backed by higher strike price puts owned. Let's assume that in early January you buy 10 XYZ July 45 puts at 4 each. In early February, XYZ is at 35. You review the put option quotations for XYZ, which are as follows:

Strike Price	April Put Option Price	July Put Option Price
40	6	6$^1/_2$
35	3	4
30	$^1/_4$	$^3/_4$

You could decide to write 10 XYZ July 35 puts at 4 each. These lower strike price puts would be completely covered through your ownership of the 10 July 45 puts. (Long higher strike price puts are approved collateral for short lower strike price puts as long as the expiration month in the short puts is the same or less distant than that of long puts. The quantity of short puts written must be equal to or less than the quantity of long puts held.)

On the sale of the 10 July 35 puts at 4 you recoup all your initial capital except for the commission costs of buying and issuing puts.

As a winning long put investor, you are now in a rather enviable position in which the most you can lose are the option commissions. Your maximum possible gain is limited to $ 10,000, less option commission.

- If at the July expiration XYZ were *over 45*, both the long 45s and the short 35s would expire worthless. You would lose the cost of the option commissions.

- If at the July expiration XYZ were *under 45 and above 35, you* would sell the long 45 puts for their intrinsic value, less the option commission. This would produce a profit for you (unless you sold the options for a small fraction). The short 35 puts would expire worthless.

- If at the July expiration XYZ were *under 35,* you would *sell* the long puts at 45 for their intrinsic value. You would *buy* the short 35 puts for their intrinsic value. You would realize a profit of $10,000 (10 x $1,000), less all option commission expense.

As in Strategy 11 for winning calls, there are many possible variations of writing short puts backed by ownership of long puts, and each choice carries with it a different risk and different reward potential. You have to make a judgment that is based on your own opinion about the underlying stock and the market at the time. Regardless of the strategy you choose, it is prudent to partially or fully hedge a winning long put option position to lock in profits or to minimize loss.

One strategy that holders of both winning put and call options should generally avoid is the exercise of their long option holdings. Exercising long calls and puts involves the following:

- Incurring stock commission expenses.
- Employing substantial additional capital.
- Taking on great additional risk.

WARNING

If you issue short calls backed by long calls with a lower strike price (for the same expiration month) and experience a price rise in the underlying stock sufficient that the short calls are trading with very little time premium over their intrinsic value (less than a half point), you should buy in the short call position and sell out the long call position to accomplish the following:

- Avoid the imminent threat of being exercised on the short call position and being forced into paying stock commissions both to buy and to sell the underlying shares.
- Cash in the near maximum profit potential.

If you issue short puts backed by long puts with a higher strike price and for the same expiration month, you should carefully watch the short put position. If the short puts go deep in the money and are trading with little time premium over their intrinsic worth (less than half a point), you should buy in the short put position and sell out the long put holding to achieve the following:

- Avoid the possibility of being exercised on the short put position and being forced to pay stock commissions to buy and to sell the underlying shares.
- Cash in the near maximum profit potential.

Lifting a leg, that is, closing one side of the position while leaving the other side open, by just buying in the short option position should also be avoided.

Buying in the short option position and remaining with the long option position does the following:

- Requires the investment of additional risk capital to effect the buy-in of the short option position.
- Exposes the long option to total risk of loss.
- Requires tremendous conviction that a truly substantial additional price move will occur in the underlying shares.

The short option "leg lifter" would have to experience a price rise in the retained long option by the amount paid to buy in the short, just to be even! An even greater price move would be needed to make the short leg lift profitable.

CHAPTER **15**

How to Figure Your Profits or Losses and the Tax Consequences

If you engage in various option strategies, you should take the time and make the effort to learn how to calculate the results of your ventures into the option world.

You should also be aware that Congress continually makes changes in the tax laws, changes that may affect option strategies as well as other investment strategies.

WARNING

It is up to each individual investor to become familiar with what the current laws are and how they may affect any contemplated investment strategy.

That advice is easy to give, it is not easy to follow. Following it requires effort, research, and decisions based on reliable sources such as IRS bulletins, tax publications, and input from CPAs who are knowledgeable about investing.

With that warning well-implanted in your mind, let's review some examples of engaging in various option strategies and the tax consequences that result under *current tax law* (subject to change by your ever-tax-concerned Congress).

Example 1

A call is written against stock bought at the exercise price, and the stock is "called away."

On February 15		On June 15	
500 XYZ bought @ 25	$12,500	500 XYZ sold by call exercise	
Plus full-service commission	+255	@ 25	$12,500
	$12,755	Less full-service commission	−255
			$12,245
5 XYZ June 25s sold @ 3	$ 1,500		
Less full-service commission	−83	Plus net call premium	+1,417
	$ 1,417	Total proceeds	$13,662
		Less net cost of stock	−12,775
		Net profit earned	$ 907

In this example:

- Profit is taxable in the year earned.
- Profit is short term (one year or less holding period).
- Profit can be used to offset carryforward capital losses from preceding years.

Before proceeding to further examples, you should try to grasp the *basic tax consequences* involved as an investor who writes, or issues, options and who buys call options.

TAX CONSEQUENCES FOR BUYERS OF CALLS

Termination

If you sell a long call option before exercise or expiration, any gain or loss is recognized as a capital gain or loss. The capital gain or loss is *long term* if the option was held more than one year or *short term* if it was held one year or less. The gain or loss is recognized in the year the call option is terminated by the sale. You may deduct *100% of net capital losses up to $3,000 per year* against highest taxed income. Any deductible losses *greater than $3,000* may be carried forward indefinitely to be used as deductions in future years or as offsets to capital gains earned.

Expiration

If a long call option *expires unexercised*, the loss is recognized as a capital loss in the year of expiration. The capital loss is long term if the option was held more than one year or short term if it was held one year or less. Net capital losses from expired long call options are fully deductible against highest taxed income *up to $3,000 in a single tax year!* Any losses *greater than the $3,000* may be carried forward to future years until used up as deductions against highest taxed income or as offsets to capital gains earned.

Exercise

If the call option is exercised by the holder of the call, the premium cost (including commission) is added to the cost of the stock purchased through the call exercise, thereby increasing the cost basis of the stock bought. There is no tax consequence until the stock is later sold.

TAX CONSEQUENCES FOR WRITERS OF CALLS

Termination

If your short call option position is eliminated through an offsetting purchase of a call option identical to the one written, any gain or loss is short-term capital gain or loss. The gain or loss will be recognized in the year of termination. This is true no matter how long the short call option position was held before termination.

Expiration

If a short (written) call option expires unexercised, the net premium initially received by the call writer is recognized as short-term capital gain in the year of expiration. This is true even if the year of expiration is a different calendar year from the year in which the premium was received.

Exercise

If a short call option is exercised against the writer of the call option, the net premium originally received is added to the net proceeds from the sale of the stock being called. The writer's cost basis is then deducted, and the resulting gain or loss is capital gain or loss. The capital gain or loss can be of long or short term, depending on how long the underlying stock was held before its sale through exercise. If the writer being called has several lots of the same stock, he or she may choose and identify the lot being delivered to the call exerciser. The writer is also free to buy new stock and to deliver that stock against the call exercise.

This freedom to select for delivery, on call exercises, between high-cost-basis stock and low-cost-basis stock is simply an extra tax management tool for the knowledgeable writer of call options.

Before going on with more examples of how to calculate profits and losses resulting from option investing, you should also become familiar with tax consequences for put buyers and for put writers.

TAX CONSEQUENCES FOR BUYERS OF PUTS

Termination

If you sell a long put option before exercise or expiration, any gain or loss is recognized as a capital gain or loss. The capital gain or loss is long term if the put was held more than one year; it is short term if the put was held one year or less. The gain or loss is recognized in the tax year the put option is terminated by the sale.

You may deduct 100% of net capital losses (up to $3,000) per year against highest taxed income. Any deductible losses greater than $3,000 may be carried forward indefinitely until used up as deductions in future years or as offsets to capital gains earned.

Expiration

If a long put expires unexercised, the loss is recognized as a capital loss in the year of expiration. The capital loss is long term if the put was held more than one year or short term if the put was held one year or less.

Net capital losses from expired long put options are fully deductible against highest taxed income up to $3,000 in a single tax year.

Any long put losses greater than $3,000 may be carried forward to future years until used up as deductions against highest-taxed income or as offsets to capital gains earned.

Exercise

If the long put option is exercised by the holder of the put, the net premium cost (including commission) is deducted from the proceeds of the net sale effected by the put exercise.

The put holder can deliver any lot of stock owned versus the sale effected by the put exercise. The put exerciser can also stipulate that the put exercise take place in a short account. You would normally attempt this strategy only if you believe that the stock will decline from the market level, at which time you could purchase low-priced shares to cover the short position.

By exercising the long put in the short stock account, the put exerciser would then be exposed to the relatively unlimited risk in the rise of the stock above the price at which the put was exercised.

TAX CONSEQUENCES FOR WRITERS OF PUTS

Termination

If your short put position is eliminated through an offsetting put purchase identical to the one written, any gain or loss is recorded as a short-term capital gain or loss. The short-term capital gain or loss is recognized in the year of termination.

Expiration

If a short put option expires unexercised, the net premium initially received by the put writer is recognized as short-term capital gain in the year the put expires. This is true even if the short put position expires after having been established for more than one year. The cost basis of an expired put is considered to be zero.

Exercise

If a short put is exercised against the writer of the put, the net premium originally received is used to reduce the cost of the stock that the put writer is obligated to purchase. There is no tax consequence until the put stock is later sold. If the put stock is sold at a later date, a capital gain or loss will be realized. The gain or loss will be short term if the put stock was sold after it was held one year or less. If the put stock were sold after being held more than one year, any gain or loss would be a long-term gain or loss.

Now that your mind is completely cluttered with the tax consequences of transacting put and call options, let's look at more examples of calculating profits or losses as a result of option activity. Maybe viewing the examples and carefully rereading the tax consequences will give you a much clearer and longer-lasting understanding of the possible outcomes of various option strategies.

Example 2

A call is written against low-cost-basis stock, and the stock is "called away."

On February 15		On June 15 XYZ is 27	
5 XYZ June 25 calls sold @ 3	$1,500	500 XYZ sold by call exercise	
Less full-service commission	–83	@ 25	$12,500
	$1,417	Less full-service commission	–255
			$12,245
500 XYZ bought @ 10		Plus net call premium	
(2 years earlier)	$5,000	received	+1,417
Plus full-service commission	+155	Total proceeds	$13,662
	$5,155	Less net cost of "old" stock	–5,155
		Net profit earned	$ 8,507

- Profit is taxable in the year the stock is called.
- Profit is long term (stock delivered was held more than two years).
- Even though the premium was short term (one year or less), it receives long-term tax treatment because it attaches to the holding period of the stock being delivered by the call exercise.

Example 3 is very complex; it involves calls issued against low-cost-basis stock. The calls are exercised, but the writer decides to keep the low-cost-basis stock and buy new shares at the market to deliver against the call exercise.

Example 3

Calls are written against low-cost-basis stock. The calls are exercised, and the writer buys new stock to deliver.

On February 15		On June 15 XYZ is 27	
5 XYZ June 15 calls sold @ 3	$1,500	500 XYZ sold by call exercise	
Less full-service commission	−83	@ 25	$12,500
Net premium received	$1,417	Less full-service commission	−255
			$12,245
500 XYZ bought @ 10			
(2 years earlier)	$5,000	Plus net call premium	
Plus full-service commission	+155	received	+1,417
	$5,155	Net sale total	$13,662
		Less 500 XYZ bought @ 27	$13,500
		Plus full-service commission	+268
		Delivered agains call exercise	
		@ 25	$13,768
		Net loss	$ 106

- The net loss of $106 is a short-term loss in the year the new stock is bought and sold via exercise of the call.
- Old low-cost-basis stock is retained, and tax liability on the gain is postponed until XYZ is later sold!
- The writer can decide to keep the low-cost-basis stock unoptioned or can write new calls at the same or higher strike price.

In Example 4, the writer issues calls against low-cost-basis stock, and the calls expire unexercised.

Example 4

Calls are written against low-cost-basis stock, and the calls expire worthless.

On February 15		On June 15 XYZ is 20	
5 XYZ June 25 calls sold @ 3	$1,500	5 XYZ June 25 calls expire	
Minus full-service commission	−83		
Net premium received	$1,417	Net premium earned	$1,417
500 XYZ bought @ 10			
(2 years earlier)	$5,000		
Plus full-service commission	+155		
	$5,155		

- Upon expiration, the net premium received is considered to be short-term capital gain earned in the year of expiration.
- The cost of expired call premiums written is considered to be zero.
- The writer can continue to hold XYZ unoptioned or can write calls at the same or different strike, as judgment dictates.

Example 5 clarifies the consequences of terminating a short call option position through an offsetting call purchase identical to the ones written.

Example 5

Calls are written against a stock purchase at the exercise price. The call obligation is terminated through an offsetting purchase.

On February 15		On April 15 XYZ is 23	
5 XYZ 25 calls sold @ 3	$ 1,500	5 XYZ June 25 calls bought @ 1	$ 500
Less full-service commission	−83	Plus full-service commission	+67
Net premium received	$ 1,417	Net premium paid	$567
500 XYZ bought @ 25	$12,500	Net premium received	$1,417
Plus full-service commission	+255	Net premium paid	−567
	$12,755	Net profit earned	$ 850

- Profit is short-term capital gain earned in the year of termination.
- The writer can continue to hold XYZ *unoptioned.*
- The writer can issue new calls at the same or different strike price and for a more distant expiration month as dictated by the investor's judgment.

In Example 6, you can observe the consequences of writing puts, the obligations of which are ended through expiration.

Example 6

Puts are written backed by U.S. Treasury Bills (T-bills), and the puts expire worthless.

On February 15 XYZ is 25		On June 15 XYZ is 27	
Sold 5 XYZ June 25 puts @ 3	$ 1,500	5 XYZ June 25 puts expire	
Less full-service commission	−83		
Net premium received	$ 1,417	Net premium earned	$ 1,417
Bought 25M T-bills due		T-bills redeemed	$25,000
June 15 at a discount	$24,500	T-bill cost	−24,565
Full-service commission		Net T-bill earnings	$ 435
to buy	+65		
	$24,565		

- The investor records short-term capital gained earned from net put premium received of $1,417.
- The cost basis of expired puts is considered to be zero.
- The gain is earned in the year of expiration.
- T-bill interest income of $435 is realized in the year bills are redeemed.

Example 7 is a little more complicated and depicts a put writer being forced to buy stock through a put exercise.

Example 7

Puts are written that are backed by T-bills. The puts are exercised.

On February 15 XYZ is 25		On June 15 XYZ is 23	
Sold 5 XYZ June puts @ 3	$ 1,500	5 XYZ June 25 puts exercised	
Minus full-service		500 XYZ bought @ 25	$12,500
commission	−83	Plus full-service commission	+755
Net put premium received	$ 1,417	Net stock cost	$13,255
Bought 25M T-bills due		Minus net put premium	
June 15 at a discount	$24,500	received	−1,417
Full-service commission		New adjusted cost price	$11,838
to buy	+65		
	$24,565	T-bills redeemed	$25,000
		T-bill cost	−24,565
		Net T-bill interest earned	$ 435

- The investor lowers the cost of stock acquired through put exercise by the net put premium received.

- There is no tax consequence until the put stock is later sold. Upon any later sale, a profit or a loss will be realized. The profit or loss will be long term if the put stock is sold more than one year after the put exercise.

- T-bill interest income of $435 is realized in the year the bills are redeemed.

It is not necessary to cite examples of every possible outcome of the implementation of an option strategy for you to be able to more clearly understand the basic tax consequences of the various option strategies and how to calculate most profits or losses that result from employing options in your investments.

You will probably need to reread and review this chapter as you begin to take part in the option universe.

If your capital permits, it would be helpful and useful for you to test various option strategies that appeal to you, doing so with a minimum amount of money. Learning by doing is still the best method of impressing the knowledge deeply into your mind.

PART TWO

Strategies Conservative Investors Should Avoid

CHAPTER 16

The Strategy of Writing Ratio Calls

Writing ratio calls is a highly sophisticated stock and option strategy that should be engaged in only by those investors who have the following characteristics:

- They are deeply knowledgeable about stocks and options.
- They understand fully the depth of risk being assumed in the naked option positions.
- They are well capitalized and prudently diversified.
- They are able to devote the time and the effort necessary to closely monitor any ratio-written situations.
- They are able to plan and execute defensive strategy in the event of adverse stock price movements.

Writing ratio calls typically involves purchasing round lots (100-share blocks) of stock and issuing a quantity of short call options that obligates the writer to deliver more shares than are currently owned.

The most common ratio write is two calls per 100 shares owned. Less aggressive ratio writers issue only four or five call options for each 300 underlying shares owned.

Whatever the ratio of your short calls to the 100-share lots of stock that you own, as long as the short calls you issue outnumber the round lots you hold, the activity is very speculative and should be avoided if you are a truly conservative investor.

Despite this admonition, many investors find themselves drawn into ratio writing by the following:

- Well-rehearsed presentations by seemingly knowledgeable sales-people.
- Articles and books that extoll the possible benefits of ratio writing.
- The investor's own seeming ability to control risk.
- The attraction of not having to guess precisely how a stock will perform within a certain time.

The mathematics of ratio writing is certainly intriguing and often does draw investors to the strategy just as moths are drawn to a flame.

To give you a better insight into writing ratio calls, we will discuss an example that should make it easier for you to understand more clearly the potential benefits of a ratio call write as well as the real risks that go hand in hand with seeking the benefits. Let's look at the most common ratio call write of two short calls per 100 shares of underlying stock owned.

Example

Let's assume that in mid-March you buy 100 XYZ at 42. The July calls for XYZ are quoted as follows:

Strike Price	Option Price
45	$2^1/2$
50	$1^1/2$

You are moderately optimistic that XYZ's price will increase by July, but you want some cash in hand in the event that a price decline in XYZ occurs.

You decide to issue two July 50 calls for $1^1/2$ each against your ownership of 100 shares. One of your objectives in issuing two calls against the 100-share position is to collect a much greater amount of cash premium than a single call would provide. That extra premium serves to provide greater insulation against a price drop.

Figure 16.1 depicts the following:

- An upside risk point at which capital should be defended to prevent the continuation of unlimited risk.
- A downside risk point at which capital might be further defended.

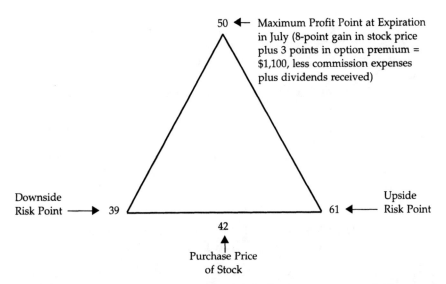

50 ← Maximum Profit Point at Expiration in July (8-point gain in stock price plus 3 points in option premium = $1,100, less commission expenses plus dividends received)

Downside Risk Point → 39

Upside 61 ← Risk Point

42

↑
Purchase Price of Stock

Figure 16.1   Ratio Write of Two Short Call Options against 100 Shares of Stock

In Figure 16. 1, 100 XYZ were bought at 42 for $4,200, and 2 XYZ July 50 calls were sold at $1½ for $300. (Commissions and dividends were omitted for simplification.) Your collection of 2 July 50 call premiums of 1½ each gives you $300 (less option commission) to protect the 100 shares you bought at 42 and to provide an extra source of return on investment.

The absolute maximum profit potential for you would occur if the stock at the July expiration was exactly 50 and both July 50 calls expired unexercised. If that happy situation occurred, you would have netted the $300 in call premiums (less the option commission), and you would be sitting on an 8-point gain on 100 shares of XYZ. At that point, several investment avenues would be open to you, as follows:

1. You could sell the 100 XYZ for a precommission gain of $800 in addition to the option profits and whatever dividends you had collected.

2. You could retain the 100 XYZ and write one new call at the 50, or higher, strike price. This would provide more money to reduce risk further.

3. You could again ratio write two calls against your 100 shares of XYZ, choosing the strike price that most nearly dovetailed with your outlook for price movement in XYZ.

When you engage in ratio writing, you establish a profit zone within which your stock can fluctuate. If, at the call expiration, the stock is above the low point in the profit zone and below the high point, you stand to benefit. The nearer to the strike price the stock price is at expiration, the greater is the benefit to the ratio writer. The establishment of this profit zone is what attracts many investors to ratio writing. With the risk points easily calculated, you can preplan defense strategies to be put into effect when those risk points are either touched or approached.

Let's now look at some of the defense strategies that you might employ if your risk points are close at hand. The figures used are from Figure 16.1.

DEFENSES FOR RATIO CALL WRITERS
AT THE UPSIDE RISK POINT

Defense I

Place a buy-stop order to purchase another 100 XYZ at 61 (or, to cover commission expenses, the buy-stop order could be at 60 or a fraction under). The buy-stop order would be executed only if the stock traded at the buy-stop price. If the buy-stop order was triggered and executed at the buy-stop price, you would be at that moment essentially at the break-even point on that particular ratio write.

There are several problems in using buy-stop orders as risk-limiting agents in writing a ratio:

• Some exchanges do not permit buy-stop orders. Exchanges that do permit buy-stop orders retain the right at any time to ban buy-stop orders. This possible ban would place you at risk of having your protective buy-stop order go unexecuted, and it would expose you to the risk of a price move above the buy-stop price.

• When and if it is executed, the buy-stop order could be at a price substantially higher than that specified in the buy-stop order, thereby placing you in a loss situation.

• The buy-stop order, even if executed exactly at the buy-stop price, places you at risk of a stock price decline below the exercise price in the short call position before the expiration date.

Defense II

Place a sell order to sell the 100 XYZ at the predetermined upside risk point (adjust the risk point to include commission expenses). If the stock sell

order is executed during the life of the short call options, you should eliminate the short calls through making offsetting purchases. The short calls at
the upside risk point would be deep in the money and usually available
with little time premium over their intrinsic value.

This defense allows the writer of the ratio call to exit entirely from
both the stock and the short call option positions at a breakeven point
or with a small loss. Any small loss taken as a result of a substantial upmove in the underlying stock in a relatively short time is quite acceptable
to most ratio writers. This is particularly so when the gain being sought
was much greater than the possible small loss anticipated. Your use of
Defense II also immediately frees up your capital for use in any other
desired investment.

As with Defense I, you may encounter problems in using Defense II to
try to limit risk in a ratio write situation.

For example, once you have sold the underlying stock at the upside
risk point, the concurrent purchase of short calls to entirely eliminate your
obligation may be executed at prices substantially higher than the intrinsic worth of the options.

You should be aware that deep-in-the-money calls are usually available at small time premiums above their intrinsic worth. "Usually" does
not mean "for sure!" Substantial time premiums over intrinsic worth sometimes occur as a result of extreme volatility in past and expected prices of
the underlying stock and in lightly traded options when the spread between the bid price and the asked price is quite wide.

DEFENSES FOR RATIO CALL WRITERS AT
THE DOWNSIDE RISK POINT

Defense I

Figure 16.1 shows that if the downside risk point of 39 is closely approached, the investor could do the following:

- Retain the 100 XYZ.

- Purchase 2 July 50 calls to eliminate the outstanding obligation.
  With a call exercise price of 50 and XYZ at 39, the calls originally
  issued for $1^1/2$ would have declined in value due to the passing of
  some time and the lower market price of XYZ.

After elimination of the obligation to deliver 200 XYZ at 50 until July expiration, you could do the following:

- Issue one new call on XYZ with a 45 strike, collecting enough premium to possibly pay all the cost of the purchase of 2 July 50s and to perhaps provide a little extra premium to pocket. Your position would change from that of a ratio writer to that of a covered call writer.

- Issue two new calls with a 45 strike for the July expiration, collecting substantially more in premium dollars than you used to purchase the 2 XYZ July 50s. You would again be in a ratio write situation but with a lower strike price.

Your decision as to whether to write calls covered or in a ratio would be influenced by your judgment of XYZ's potential from the new lower price level.

Defense II

If the July 50 calls originally issued for $1^{1/2}$ each decline to a small fraction ($3/8$ to $1/4$), you may decide to defend your capital by doing one of the following:

- Sell 100 XYZ.
- Buy 2 XYZ July 50 calls, eliminating the obligation completely.
- Reinvest the net proceeds in a different stock or other investment.

This defense normally would be used only if you develop a changed and negative opinion about XYZ and its potential for price recovery. Any loss sustained in exiting from the ratio write situation should be small.

Each defense at a particular risk point has its own advocates. There is no one particular defense that you can always select as the right one to use. You simply have to make a case-by-case judgment. Your ability to make those judgments is aided by experience from the hands-on managing of your assets.

Those investors who obtain sufficient experience and still continually lose money or earn very little on their investments should consider leaving the field to others whose abilities are more proficient. Ratio writing is simply not for the faint of heart, the inept investor, or the conservative investor.

WARNINGS

- Investors who decide to engage in writing ratio calls should be sufficiently well capitalized as to have reserve funds available to completely pay for any shares purchased at the upside risk point.
- Investors who decide to engage in writing ratio calls should focus on writing out-of-the-money calls so that the upside risk point that might be defended is substantially higher than the current market price of shares bought. For writers of ratio calls, the upside risk point involves a much greater threat of capital loss than does the downside risk point. Therefore, the upside risk point should be placed further from the strike price than the downside risk point.

CHAPTER 17

The Strategy of Writing Ratio Puts

One of the more esoteric and intriguing of the investment strategies involving both stocks and options is the *shorting* of stock versus the issuing of puts that obligate the investor to buy a greater number of shares than the quantity sold short (shorted).

This is certainly a strategy that conservative investors should avoid! Yet this strategy is essentially a mirror image of writing ratio calls, which was discussed in the preceding chapter. In fact, the risk and the rewards to investors employing this strategy in many ways parallel those of the writer of ratio calls.

In one of the most popular ratio call writes, the investor buys 100 shares of a stock and issues two call options. A profit zone is thereby created within which the stock can fluctuate and still reward the investor with a profit. Profits are attainable as long as the stock remains above the downside risk point and below the upside risk point.

This particular concept is suitable only for very speculative, aggressive investors steeped in option knowledge as well as in the fundamentals of the underlying stock. Despite the riskiness of the strategy, otherwise conservative investors are often tempted to test the strategy because they think they have the ability to control risk and because of the mathematics and reward potential of the profit zone. As popular as ratio call writing is among investors, ratio put writing attracts few adherents.

To help you better understand ratio put writing, I have created two illustrations that should help shed some light on the strategy and how it differs from ratio call writing.

Example 1

Let's assume that in mid-March you sell short 100 XYZ at 42. The July put options for XYZ are quoted as follows:

Strike Price	Option Price
40	$2^1/_2$
45	5

Notice carefully that the July 40 put is an out-of-the-money put and that the July 45 put is an in-the-money put.

You decide to sell short 100 XYZ at 42. Against this short position you issue 2 July 45 puts at 5 each. This gives you $1,000 in advance cash (less option commission) to protect against an advance in the price of XYZ.

Figure 17.1 shows the following:

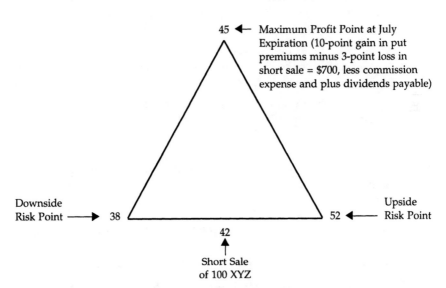

45 ← Maximum Profit Point at July Expiration (10-point gain in put premiums minus 3-point loss in short sale = $700, less commission expense and plus dividends payable)

Downside Risk Point → 38

Upside Risk Point ← 52

42
↑
Short Sale of 100 XYZ

Figure 17.1   Ratio Write of Two In-the-Money Short Puts versus 100 Shares of Stock Sold Short

- An upside risk point at which you should defend your capital to prevent the continuation of unlimited risk.
- A downside risk point at which you might also defend your capital against further price erosion.

In Figure 17.1, 100 XYZ sold short at 42 for $4,200, and 2 XYZ July 45 puts sold at 5 each for $1,000. (Commissions and dividends payable were omitted for simplification.) The collection of 2 July 45 put premiums of $500 each provides you with $1,000 to protect against a price rise in the100 XYZ short positions and provides a potential source of profit.

Your absolute maximum profit potential would be at the July expiration if XYZ were exactly 45 and both July 45 puts expired unexercised. If that situation did occur, you would net the $1,000 in put premiums (less option commissions). You would be sitting with an unrealized loss of $300 from your short sale at 42. At that point, you could pursue any one of the following investment alternatives:

- You could buy 100 XYZ at 45 and close out the short sale, losing $300. The $1,000 premium you received from the puts would cover the loss, the commission expense, and any normal dividends paid while short, and it would still provide a profit.
- You could keep the 100-share XYZ short position and write one new put at a strike price that meshed with your judgment of the future price action in XYZ.
- You could again ratio write two puts against your 100-share short position, thereby collecting another round of premium dollars to insulate against the risk.

You should be cognizant of the similarities between buying 100 XYZ and issuing two calls and selling short 100 XYZ and issuing two puts. In both strategies, you:

- Bear the risk of a price rise in 100 XYZ that theoretically is unlimited.
- Bear the risk of a price fall in 100 XYZ down to zero.
- Collect two advance premiums to soften the rise or the fall.

There are four substantial differences between ratio call writing and ratio put writing that investors engaging in the activity should know:

1.   To sell short, you must first arrange to borrow the shares to be sold short. This is not always possible.

2.   If you are selling shares short, you must pay any cash or stock dividends or distributions that go exdividend during the life of the short position.

3.   Even though you may be able to borrow shares to sell short, there is absolutely no assurance that you can hold the borrowed shares to the expiration of the put obligations. The lender of the shares has the right to demand return of the shares at any time, which could force you into liquidating the short stock positions at an inopportune time not of your own choosing.

4.   Sellers of short stock must also realize that exchange rules require that any short stock sales be executed on an uptick. (An *uptick* is a price that is higher than the last different price.) This restriction may prevent the execution of a short stock sale at a price considered attractive by the short seller.

When you engage in ratio put writing, you establish a profit zone within which the stock can fluctuate and still produce a profit for you. If at the put expiration the stock is above the downside risk point (adjusted for commissions) and below the upside risk point (also adjusted for commissions), you stand to benefit. The nearer to the strike price that the stock price is at expiration, the greater is the benefit to the ratio put writer.

Example 2

In Figure 17.2, 100 XYZ sold short at 42 for $4,200, and 2 XYZ July 40 puts sold at 2¹/₂ each for $500. (Commissions and dividends payable were omitted for simplification.)

In Figure 17.2, the put writer can also earn interest on the collateral used to back the puts and the short sale, as well as on interest earned on the advance put premiums received.

Using the situation in Figure 17.2, you decide to sell short 100 XYZ at 42. Against this short position, you issue 2 July 40 puts at 2¹/₂ each. This provides you with $500 in advance cash (less option commission) to protect against a price advance in XYZ. Your absolute maximum profit potential at the July expiration would be for XYZ to be exactly 40 and for both July 40 puts to expire unexercised.

If both July 40 puts expired unexercised, you would net $500 in put premiums (less option commission). You would be sitting with an unreal-

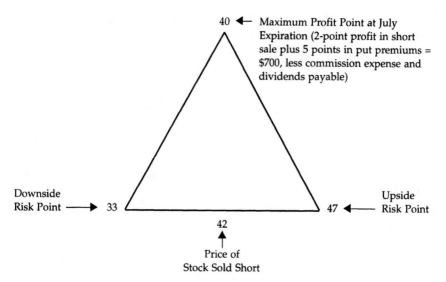

40 ← Maximum Profit Point at July
      Expiration (2-point profit in short
      sale plus 5 points in put premiums =
      $700, less commission expense and
      dividends payable)

Downside   Upside
Risk Point ──→ 33   47 ←── Risk Point

42
↑
Price of
Stock Sold Short

Figure 17.2   Ratio Write of Two Out-of-the-Money Short Puts versus 100 Shares of Stock Sold Short

ized gain of $200 from the short stock sale at 42. At that point, you could pursue one of the following investment alternatives:

- You could buy 100 XYZ at 40 to cover the short sale at 42. This would create $200 in precommission profits to go with $500 in precommission option premiums earned.

- You could remain short 100 XYZ and write one new put at the strike price that most meshed with your opinion of the future price action in XYZ.

- You could again ratio write two new puts against the 100 short position in XYZ. The strike selected for the new puts issued would be based on your judgment of the price movement that might take place in XYZ.

Any investor entering into ratio put writing should certainly give considerable thought to executing a defensive strategy should XYZ closely approach either the upside risk point or the downside risk point.

Some of the defensive strategies that you might employ as a ratio put writer are discussed.

DEFENSES FOR RATIO PUT WRITERS
AT THE UPSIDE RISK POINT

Defense I

Place a buy-stop order to purchase 100 XYZ at the upside risk point (adjusted for commission expenses). If the order is executed, you can use that stock to close out the short sale. At the same time you buy the stock, eliminate the two short puts with offsetting purchases.

With the puts far out of the money, your cost to cancel the obligations should be relatively small. Closing all positions when the upside risk point is breached normally creates a relatively small loss.

Buy-stop orders, however, have several accompanying risks, which are detailed in the preceding chapter. Review these risks carefully before you enter into a ratio writing situation that would require you to use a buy-stop order as a capital defense tactic. In executing Defense I, you would have extracted your capital and would be able to reinvest it in other situations.

Defense II

With XYZ closely approaching the upside risk point, the short puts you originally issued would be far out of the money and would have lost the major part of their value. You could eliminate the put obligations through offsetting purchases, producing a net profit from the options transactions.

You could issue a new put or two new puts (depending on your outlook for XYZ) at a strike price near the upside risk point. This action would bring in additional funds to help cushion the existing loss in the 100 shares of XYZ you sold short. This defense leaves you at risk of a continued large move up by XYZ or a large move down by XYZ.

DEFENSES FOR RATIO PUT WRITERS
AT THE DOWNSIDE RISK POINT

Defense I

With the downside risk point being closely approached, you could buy 100 shares of XYZ and use those shares to close out the short stock sale at a profit. That profit plus the net put option premiums you initially collected would serve to cushion any stock loss incurred by an exercise of the two puts. Upon closing the short sale at a profit, you would no longer be exposed to any upside risk in XYZ. You would hope that after the short stock sale closing, XYZ would rally back to the put strike price or above. If that happened, you could do one of the following:

- Opt to sell 100 XYZ short again versus the two still outstanding put obligations and hope for another price drop after the second short stock sale was executed.
- Hope that XYZ would be above the put exercise price at the July expiration, which would allow you to net the initial put premiums (less option commission) in addition to the profit garnered on the earlier closing of the short stock sale.

Defense II

With XYZ near the downside risk point, you could decide to buy 100 XYZ and use those shares to close the short stock sale at a profit. Simultaneously with the purchase of XYZ stock, you could purchase two in-the-money puts to cancel the ones previously issued. These purchases would normally return to you the bulk of the funds you initially used to enter the ratio put situation. The losses sustained on exiting the situation would normally be relatively small.

In my view, writing ratio puts should be entered into only by investors who meet the following qualifications:

- They are aggressive risk takers.
- They are fully versed in option strategy.
- They have the time and make the effort to closely monitor all outstanding short stock and short put positions.
- They fully reserve the funds that may become necessary as a result of any short put exercises.
- They are disciplined decision makers.

Ratio put writing at best is a very stressful and complicated way of seeking profits. As the saying goes, "Forewarned is forearmed!"

CHAPTER 18

The Naked Call Writing Strategy

Each bear market in stocks seems to bring a substantial increase in naked call writing. This strategy has a magnetic appeal for a large group of sophisticated investors who have great determination to beat the game. *Naked call writing*, for the uninitiated, is an option strategy wherein the investor issues call options without any direct or indirect ownership in the underlying securities.

The brokerage firms that permit investors to issue naked calls try to protect the capital of the firm (which guarantees the delivery of securities subject to the call exercise) in the event of a default by the writer by requiring the naked call writer to have on deposit with the firm some sort of collateral, such as bonds (corporate, municipal, or U.S. government), other marginal stocks or mutual funds, Treasury bills, or cash. The collateral requirements vary from firm to firm, and they are usually in excess of the minimum margin specified by the Federal Reserve and the various exchanges. The collateral requirement is much less than that needed to buy stock on margin.

Whatever the collateral requirements to write naked calls, many aggressive and sophisticated investors who engage in the strategy are attracted by the following characteristics:

- The high degree of leverage.
- The avoidance of any stock commission expense for every correct judgment.
- The possibility of high percentage returns in short periods.
- The desire to test their market judgment of a particular stock or stocks.
- The relative short period of risk exposure.

Naked call writing ranks right at the top of option investment strategies that are labeled *high risk*. No conservative investor should even *experiment* in writing naked calls. The practice is better left to those willing to risk financial suicide in return for highly leveraged profits.

If you issue naked calls, you are agreeing to expose your deposited capital and other assets to *unlimited risk* and to accept *very limited amounts* of advance cash in return for the great risk incurred.

If the foregoing makes you wonder why investors participate in writing naked calls, perhaps a couple of examples will help you gain at least an understanding. You should also understand that naked call writers are bearish on the outlook for a price rise in the stock underlying the naked calls they issue.

The typical naked calls writer normally focuses his or her naked call writing attention on (1) out-of-the-money calls and (2) calls with short periods until expiration.

Example 1

Assume that it is mid-March. You look at XYZ priced at 42. The market is "weak."

Stock Price Year Hi–Lo	Call Strike Price	April Call Price
50–35	45	1¹/₂
	50	¹/₂

You have studied XYZ's fundamentals and believe that sales and earnings are heading down. A dividend cut is likely.

You have $100,000 invested in Treasury bills that earn an annual rate of 6%. Afflicted with an attack of greed and a negative view toward XYZ, you decide to issue 10 naked calls on XYZ. Following your very bearish opinion on XYZ, you write 10 April 45s at 1¹/₂ each.

- You collected $1,380 after full-service option commission expense.
- The Treasury bills are sufficient collateral to permit you to issue 10 naked April 45s.
- You are exposed to risk should a large percentage upside move above 45 occur during the one-month life of the call option (mid-March to mid-April).

- Should your judgment prove correct and the 10 April 45s expire unexercised, the $1,380 you have earned would represent a 23% increase in the $6,000 annual earnings of the Treasury bills—an increase earned in a single month!

Certainly investors who do incur the risk in writing naked calls should place limits where defensive action will be taken to try to contain the unlimited risk to which their capital is exposed. In Example 1, you could try to protect your capital by buying 10 April 45 calls (to eliminate your naked position) if and when XYZ sells at 46. With the stock at 46, the April 45s would be in the money and normally could be purchased for very little time premium over the intrinsic worth of $1. If you effected this closing purchase, you would about break even on the options transaction. Breaking even would be a good result for a stock misjudgment that saw a price advance of approximately 10% in 30 days, instead of an expected flat to down movement.

In most instances this loss-limiting technique works satisfactorily, but it does have the following disadvantages:

- It requires constant monitoring by you or your account executive.
- If buy-stop orders are used (where permitted), they might be executed far above the buy-stop price.
- A halt in trading of XYZ accompanied by a takeover announcement at a price much higher than the actual or the mental buy-stop price could cause you to incur a severe loss.

Some very thoughtful and experienced writers of naked calls try to avoid unexpected upward price movements caused by a takeover announcement by restricting their writes of naked calls to stocks judged by them to be "takeover-proof "—such as giant utilities and giant industrials (for example, General Motors and IBM).

Another method that writers of naked calls often employ to contain risk is to issue calls that are so far out of the money as to require a very large percentage of gain just to reach the strike price of the calls. If they can couple the high percentage requirement with a short period to expiration, they feel that the mathematical probabilities are heavily weighted in favor of the writer of the naked call.

Be aware that historical studies conducted by leading option exchanges show that the great bulk of far-out-of-the-money calls with short periods to expiration do expire worthless.

Despite the encouragement of positive statistics, one big loss can wipe out all the winnings of a writer's naked calls and seriously erode the writer's capital. Writing naked calls is simply better left to the following:

- The well-capitalized, extremely well-informed speculative investor.

- Option strategists who broadly diversify.

- Investors with quick and easy access to prompt executions that are often required to contain risk.

- Decisive investors with an insurance-company mind who believe the collection of many small premiums will outweigh the occasional large loss.

Now let's look at another possible situation.

Example 2

With $100,000 invested in Treasury bills earning 6% annually, you have a bearish outlook for the price movement in XYZ from mid-March to mid-April. To protect against a possible wrong judgment of XYZ, you decide to issue 10 XYZ April 50s for $1/2$ each. XYZ is at 42 at the time you issue the naked call.

- You collected $435 (after full-service option commission expense) from the sale of 10 April 50s at $1/2$.

- You continue to earn 6% annually on the $100,000 in Treasury bills that serve as collateral for the naked calls you issued.

- In the one month remaining in the call option's life, XYZ would have to move from the current price of 42 to above 50 to place you at risk.

- Should your judgment prove to be correct and the 10 April 50s expire unexercised, the $435 would represent a $7^1/4$% increase in the annual $6,000 earnings of the $100,000 Treasury bills held—an increase that was earned in a single month!

Readers should note that writers of naked far-out- of-the-money calls can afford to misjudge a stock's upside move potential within the period of the naked call by the difference between the market price of the stock and the strike price in the calls and can still win the entire advance premium collected!

This margin for error is simply another attractive feature that entices many investors into writing naked calls that are far out of the money. Readers should also carefully note the following:

- The risk in writing naked calls, although theoretically unlimited, in actual practice is limited. This is because either the investor will take a defensive action to contain the risk or the brokerage firm will buy in the investor's obligations to protect the brokerage firm from financial harm. The brokerage firm's buy-in procedures usually take effect when the investor's collateral value has been eroded beyond the minimum maintenance margin that the firm requires of writers of naked calls.

- There are times, however, when a price upmove is so rapid and so large that the buy-in cannot be executed in time to prevent the writer's collateral from being completely dissipated, along with some of the brokerage firm's own capital. The brokerage firm holds the client liable for losses the firm sustains and must collect from the client if possible.

- If the naked call writer's bearish opinion of XYZ is borne out by a severe drop in XYZ's price, the maximum that can ever be earned from the correct analysis is the relatively small amount of premium dollars initially collected.

- A writer of a naked call whose option obligations go from out of the money at the time of the call issuance to significantly in the money runs the additional risk of being exercised. Being exercised forces the writer to incur stock commission expenses to sell the stock and stock commission expenses to buy the stock being called. Any loss is enhanced by the additional burden of the stock commissions.

In my opinion, the benefits that might be obtained through writing naked calls are far outweighed by the severity of the risk assumed. Most investors would be well advised to read about and to understand naked call writing but not to participate in the strategy.

CHAPTER 19

The Calendar Spread Strategy

Listed stock option trading offers an almost unlimited variety of investment strategies for seeking profits while holding risk in check and holding it to a predeterminable amount.

One of the most interesting of those strategies to very aggressive speculative investors is *calendar spreads*. Calendar spreads in the option world are also known as *horizontal spreads*.

Calendar call option spreads involve purchasing calls and reducing the risk in the purchased calls by selling calls under the following conditions:

- At the same strike price as those owned.
- With an expiration date shorter than the date of the calls owned.
- On the same underlying stock as in the calls owned.

This fascinating option strategy has several attractive features that exert a tremendous pull on investors to try the strategy on an underlying stock on which they have formed some definite opinions as to possible price action in the shares. The most attractive features of calendar call option spreads are the following:

- An extremely high degree of leverage is obtained.
- The short call premiums collected can be immediately used to offset the cost of the long calls purchased.
- The long calls serve as margin collateral for the short calls issued and as insurance that limits the risk in the short call position.

- The profit potential under certain circumstances may become *unlimited.*
- The risk can be absolutely fixed and is known in advance.

To engage in calendar spreading, you must meet certain requirements of the firm that is going to execute orders for your account. Among the requirements are the following:

- A financial statement of your liquid assets.
- A statement that speculation or aggressive investing is a primary investment objective.
- Sufficient margin collateral to meet the minimums established by the Federal Reserve and the extra collateral required by the brokerage firm.
- A history of previous investment experience.

Example

Let's suppose you have decided to give calendar call option spreading a try. You open an account at a brokerage firm after meeting all the firm's requirements.

You have carefully analyzed XYZ stock and have formed the opinion that XYZ's near-term price action could be slightly up or down as a result of rather static current quarter earnings and sales projections. The coming quarter should show much higher sales and earnings, you believe. Armed with that information, you peruse the quoted call option prices on XYZ.

In mid-March XYZ is at 42, and XYZ call options are as follows:

Strike Price	April Call Price	July Call Price
45	$3/4$	2
50	$1/4$	$7/8$

You decide to do the following:

Buy 20 XYZ July 45s @ 2	$4,000
Plus full-service commission	+208
Net purchase cost	$4,208

Sell 20 XYZ April 45s @ 3/4	$1,500
Minus full-service commission	−150
Net sale receipt	$1,350

You are allowed to apply option sale proceeds against the cost of the option purchase cost. Your out-of-pocket cost on entering into the calendar call option spread would be $2,858 ($4,208 − $1,350).

PROFIT POSSIBILITIES

Now let's take a look at the possibilities for profit in the spread.

Profit Possibility I

XYZ remains under 45 through the April expiration. The short XYZ 45 calls die worthless, because your expectations for the stock price for XYZ shares are borne out. You still own 20 XYZ July 45s with three months of life remaining in which an upward price move might take place. At the July expiration, the 20 XYZ calls still held would be worth:

Some XYZ Possible Prices	Value of 20 XYZ Calls
Under 45	0
50	$10,000 (less commission)
55	20,000 (less commission)
60	30,000 (less commission)
70	50,000 (less commission)

The profit potential above the $45 level is theoretically unlimited.

Profit Possibility II

As a very venturesome horizontal call option spreader, you paid 1 1/4 (2 to 3/4) points difference per spread to enter into the spread situation. You would profit if the spread difference widened in your favor to a point at which you could liquidate both sides of the spread for a greater difference than originally expensed—a difference large enough to produce a profit after all commission expenses involved.

Assume that in early April, XYZ has advanced from the spread entry level of 42 to 44 and that XYZ call option prices are quoted as follows:

Strike Price	April Call Price	July Call Price
45	$1/4$	$2^1/2$

You could liquidate both sides of the spread as follows:

Buy 20 XYZ April 45s @ $1/4$	$ 500
Plus full-service commission	+62
Net purchase cost	$ 562
Sell 20 XYZ July 45s @ $2^1/2$	$5,000
Less full-service commission	−220
Net sale proceeds	$4,780
Net spread liquidation proceeds	$4,218
Initial out-of-pocket spread cost	−2,858
Net gain on the spread trades	$1,360

The $1,360 spread profit represents a 47.5% return on your investment—a return earned in less than three weeks! It is not surprising that a great number of risk-oriented investors "test" call option spreading.

THE RISKS OF CALENDAR CALL OPTION SPREADS

Now that you have seen the profit potentials for call option calendar spreads, you should carefully review the risks.

Risk I

One risk that you must bear when you engage in calendar call option spreads is that both the short call option you issue and the long call option you own may expire unexercised and worthless. In that event, you would experience the total loss of the net amount you have invested in the spread difference. Using the figures from our initial call option spread illustration:

- The 20 XYZ April 45s sold at $3/4$ for $1,350 (net after option commission) die worthless.

- The 20 XYZ July 45s bought at 2 for $4,208 (net after option commission) die worthless.

You record as a tax-deductible loss, the net difference of $2,858 ($4,208–$1,350).

Risk II

Another risk that you bear as a calendar call option spread investor is that the underlying stock may rise sufficiently in price to send your call options deep in the money. With the call options now deep in the money, there is a very real danger that your short call position will be exercised.

If that unhappy event occurs, you will be forced to sell the underlying shares required by the contract and expense the commission cost incurred in the sale of the shares. To fulfill the delivery obligation, you will have to choose from several possible courses of action, as follows:

- Exercise the long calls you own to get the shares you need to deliver against the short call exercise, expensing the additional commission cost of buying the shares.

- Buy the required shares in the open market and deliver those versus the short call exercise, expensing the additional commission cost of buying the shares. You could retain the long calls you own and hope for a continued rise.

- Buy the required shares in the open market and deliver those versus the short call exercise, expensing the additional commission cost of buying the shares. You would then sell the long calls you own to capture whatever time premium exists over the intrinsic in-the-money worth.

- Have the proceeds of the sale of stock that resulted from the short call exercise placed in a short account. If you request this special treatment, you must have other securities in the account with sufficient collateral value to permit placing the proceeds of the stock sale into the short account.

Using the figures from our previous illustration, upon being called your situation would be as follows:

Short 2,000 XYZ shares @ 45	$90,000
Less full-service commission	–932
Net sale proceeds	$89,068

Long 20 XYZ July 45 call options with more than three months of remaining life.

Your hope is that before the July expiration, XYZ will decline far enough below 45 so that you can buy 2,000 XYZ and use it to close out the short stock position. That would leave you with a profit after paying stock commission expenses to buy and to sell. You would still be left owning 20 XYZ July 45 calls that you could use again to go deep in the money and provide another liquidating profit. The likelihood of such a scenario actually taking place is remote but certainly possible.

Let's take a worst-case look at the risk involved. Let's say that you do the following:

Sell 20 April 45s @ 3/4	$1,500
Less full-service commission	−150
Net call sale proceeds	$1,350
Buy 20 July 45s @ 2	$4,000
Plus full-service commission	+208
Net purchase call	$4,208

You would be risking the following:

- A net spread difference of $2,858.
- Plus stock commission expenses of $1,864 stemming from an early exercise of the short April 45s, forcing an exercise of the long July 45s to meet your obligation.
- A total potential loss of $4,722 ($2,858 + $1,864).

As you are sure to notice, the original spread difference risk of $2,858 grew to $4,722 through having to expense stock commission expenses due to exercising of both the short and the long call positions.

GUIDE RULES FOR CALENDAR CALL OPTION SPREADS

If you are an investor with a speculative bent who wishes to test your luck at the wheel, I have guide rules for calendar call option spreads that should provide you with the best opportunity for a successful outcome from the venture.

Rule I

Enter into calendar call option spreads only when both the short call and the long call are out of the money.

Rule II

Select underlying stocks on which you have carefully reviewed the fundamentals and have formed an opinion that the strike price in the short call with the near-term expiration is not likely to be penetrated.

Rule III

Be prepared to exit from both sides of the spread should the call options go deep in the money or in the money to the extent that the near-term short call carries very little time premium over the intrinsic worth of the call. Exercises of short call positions can be extremely costly to the spreader.

Rule IV

Avoid selecting any stock for a call option calendar spread that is labeled as a takeover candidate or has most of the characteristics associated with takeover candidates.

Rule V

Investors engaging in calendar call option spreading should negotiate substantial commission discounts from a full-service firm or execute the spread orders through a traditional discount firm.

Call option calendar spreading is a strategy that simply is not one for conservative investors to use. It is a speculative venture with many attractive features for the following kinds of investors:

- Quick-witted, decisive investors seeking highly leveraged profit opportunities.
- Investors wanting to test their judgment of a stock's price movement over a relatively short period with the risk being restricted to a predeterminable amount.
- Investors who are informed about option strategy and who can maintain close supervision of their option positions. (You don't want to be on an African safari if you are holding open spread positions.)

CHAPTER 20

The Call Option Butterfly Spread Strategy

The number and variety of option strategies that can be used to seek profits and to contain risk are almost mind-boggling.

Among the most esoteric, sophisticated, and difficult to understand and to execute is a strategy called the *butterfly spread*. Butterfly spreads can be constructed for either put options or call options. To help you in the burdensome task of trying to get a grasp on and to assimilate the various strategies that exist, the examples in this chapter detail the call option butterfly spread.

The call option butterfly spread involves the speculative investor in executing call options with three different exercise (strike) prices, on the same underlying stock, and for the same expiration month.

Each call option butterfly spread consists of the following parts:

- One long, low strike price call option.
- Two short, middle strike price call options.
- One long, high strike price call option.

Speculators who like to take high risks try to wrest profits from call option butterfly spreads because they perceive the following advantages:

- The risk has definite and predeterminable limits.
- The profit potential can range from moderate to high.
- Flexibility is great because butterfly spreads can be constructed for expected downmoves or upmoves in the underlying stock price.
- The zone in which a profit may be extracted is wide.

- Precise pinpoint estimation of the underlying stock's price movement within the period of the spread of the option is not required in order to win.

HOW BUTTERFLY SPREADS WORK

Let's take a look at how call option butterfly spreads work.

Example

You, our heroic speculator (one must be brave and somewhat masochistic to seek profits in this particular strategy), are drawn by the advantages in call option spreading, and you spot an apparent opportunity for a call option butterfly spread that is based on the following option price quotations in early April:

Strike Price	July Call Option Price
110	15 (in-the-money call)
120	10 (at-the-money call)
130	6 (out-of-the-money call)

XYZ is currently priced at 120 per share. XYZ is a highly regarded volatile stock in the computer industry. You place orders with your broker to do the following:

Buy 5 XYZ July 110s @ 15	$ 7,500
Plus full-service commission	+155
Net purchase cost	$ 7,655
Sell 10 XYZ July 120s @ 10	$10,000
Less full-service commission	−225
Net sale proceeds	$ 9,775
Buy 5 XYZ July 130s @ 6	$ 3,000
Plus full-service commission	+105
Net purchase cost	$ 3,105

Your long call positions expense is $10,760 ($7,655 + $3,105); your short call position proceeds are $9,775; and your total initial out-of-pocket cash invested in the call option butterfly spreads is $985 ($10,760 − $9,775).

With your position established, let's look at some possible outcomes at the July expiration.

Possible Outcome I

At the July expiration, XYZ is below 110, which is the lowest strike price. The following will expire worthless:

- 5 long calls at 110.
- 10 short calls at 120.
- 5 long calls at 130.

You will record a tax-deductible loss of $985, which represents your total out-of-pocket cash (including commissions) invested in the call option butterfly spreads.

Possible Outcome II

At the July expiration, XYZ is at 120, which is the middle strike price in your call option butterfly spread. The following will occur:

- 5 long calls at 110 would be sold for their intrinsic worth of 10 calls for $5,000.
- 10 short calls at 120 would expire worthless.
- 5 long calls at 130 would also expire worthless.

Your net proceeds from exiting all parts of the call option butterfly spread are $4,873; your net out-of-pocket cash used to enter into the call option butterfly spread is $985; and your net gain after all commission expenses is $3,888.

Notice that your optimum profit for call option butterfly spreads is *always at the middle strike price.*

Table 20.1   Butterfly Spreads

The 5 long calls @ 110 would be sold for their intrinsic value of 20.	$10,000
Less full-service commission	−185
Net sale proceeds	$ 9,815
The 10 short calls @ 120 would be bought for their intrinsic value of 10.	$10,000
Plus full-service commission	+225
Net purchase cost	$10,225
The 5 long calls @ 130 would die worthless.	$ 0

Possible Outcome III

At the July expiration, XYZ is at 130, which is the high strike price in your call option butterfly spread. The events given in Table 20.1 will occur.

The net result of your exiting from the call option butterfly spread would be as follows:

Initial out-of-pocket spread entry cost	$ 985
Purchase of 10 short 120 calls to cancel obligation	+10,225
	$11,210
Sales proceeds from liquidating 5 long 110 calls	−9,815
Net tax-deductible loss on exiting the call option butterfly spread	$ 1,395

In the real option investment world, you would normally exit from the spread when the short middle strike calls went deep in the money and were trading with little time premium over their intrinsic worth. This forced exit could take place through a sharp upmove by XYZ long before the July expiration.

The possibility of the deep-in-the-money short call options being exercised before the expiration date would be a very real threat. If an exercise did take place, you would bear the financial burden of having to pay stock commission expenses to sell 1,000 XYZ at 120 as per your obligation. You would also have to pay stock commission expense to buy 1,000 shares of XYZ by exercising the five 110 strike price calls held and by either buying 500 XYZ in the market or exercising the five 130 strike price calls held.

In the foregoing illustration your profit zone (theoretically) would extend from above 110 to under 130, with the optimum profit being realized at the middle strike price at expiration.

DISADVANTAGES OF CALL OPTION BUTTERFLY SPREADING

To me the disadvantages that accompany call option butterfly spreading so far outweigh the advantages that the activity should be avoided by almost all investors.

Let's examine these disadvantages so that you will at least be well enough informed to resist any sales presentation that is heavily accented toward the pluses of call option butterfly spreading.

Disadvantage I: Problems in Order Execution

Call option butterfly spreaders find it very difficult to get orders executed at prices that are close to the apparent values as reflected by the last prices of the calls under consideration. We will use the same prices used in the preceding example of XYZ call options:

Strike Price	July Call Option Price	Bid–Asked
110	15	$14^1/2$ to $15^1/2$
120	10	$9^3/4$ to $10^1/4$
130	6	$5^3/4$ to $6^1/4$

If you want quick entry into the call option butterfly spread, you would have to do the following:

- Buy 5 July 110s at the asked price of $15^1/2$ each.
- Sell 10 July 120s at the bid price of $9^3/4$ each.
- Buy 5 July 130s at the asked price of $6^1/4$ each.

These actions would substantially increase your spread entry cost over the cost shown in our example that was based on last sale prices (page 154).

Entering call option butterfly spread orders at the market from last price is a very risky venture. My advice is to never enter into call option spread orders at the market.

Call option butterfly spreaders generally enter into the spread in one of two ways:

1. Through orders specifying that orders involving three different strike prices, two long call positions, and one short call position

be executed at a specified net debit or net credit exclusive of commission costs.

2. Through legging into the call option butterfly spread.

The prices at which the options are purchased and sold do not matter as long as the net credit or net debit is as specified or better. Using the last sale price in our example:

Strike Price	July Call Option Last Sale
110	15
120	10
130	6

A single call option butterfly spread would consist of:

- 1 long July 110
- 2 short July 120s
- 1 long July 130

The long 110 and the long 130, if purchased at the last price, would cost $21 (15 + 6). The sale of the 2 short 120s at 10 each would bring $20. Applying the sales proceeds against the purchase cost would create a precommission debit of 1 per call option butterfly spread executed.

Using the *net debit* or *net credit order entry* at least assures you that any spreads executed will be exactly as you wish or better.

Exiting from call option butterfly spreads can also be done with net debit or net credit orders. However, if there is a definite threat of an exercise as a result of the short call options going deep in the money, the exit from the spread should be accomplished with market orders to prevent the incurrence of stock commission expenses.

Legging into the call option butterfly spread is often used by many players of the game. Their method usually involves purchasing first the lower strike price calls. Then, if they get a move up in the underlying stock after the purchase of the low strike price calls, they sell the middle strike price calls at a price usually greater than they could have realized at the time they purchased the low strike price calls. Simultaneously with the sale of the middle strike price calls, they buy the high strike price calls thereby capping their risk to any total spread debit incurred, plus commission expenses. Of course, the legger runs the risk after the first leg purchase that the other legs may not be put on as a result of a sharp downmove in the stock.

The call option butterfly spreader's dream deal is to get into a call option butterfly sandwich spread *even*. That would happen if the money collected from the sale of the middle strike calls equaled the money expensed for the purchase of the protective low and high strike price calls.

Disadvantage II: Commission Expenses

The second disadvantage of engaging in call option butterfly spreads is the extremely high commission costs incurred in pursuing a limited profit. Each call option butterfly spread entered into entails four option commissions. Getting out of the spread could also entail up to four more option commissions or, in the event of an exercise against the short call position, high stock commission expenses.

Disadvantage III: Limited Profit Potential

In a call option butterfly spread, the maximum profit potential at expiration is at the middle strike price. That maximum generally:

- Has a low probability of occurring.
- Is not worth the high expenses incurred.
- Is not worth the constant monitoring and supervision that are required.
- Is not worth the risk of being forced out of the position early in the life of the spreads because of a strong stock price upmove that brings forth the threat of exercise.

Call option butterfly spreading is a strategy best left to truly sophisticated optionwise investors who pay little or no commissions on their option trades because of their ownership or memberships on an option exchange.

Call option butterfly spreads are well known in the securities industry by another name: *alligator spreads*. That name was ascribed to the strategy by some wit who reasoned that the commissions can eat an investor alive.

If you do seek profits through call option butterfly spreads, you will be loved by the broker handling your account (assuming you are being "helped" by a full-service firm representative). And you will be valued highly by the brokerage firm executing your orders.

CHAPTER 21

Married Puts: An Expensive Wedding between Stock and Option

Investors delving into the strategies of the option world are frequently attracted to a strategy known by the unusual name of *married put*. On the surface, this strategy offers tremendous appeal to buyers of common stock through the insurance provided by a put purchase. The married put strategy involves you in the following process:

- Purchasing a round lot of an optionable common stock.
- Purchasing a put option the same day of the stock purchase, and on the same stock.
- Identifying the put as a hedge for the just-purchased stock.
- Increasing the purchase cost of the stock by the amount of the put.

The theory of the married put strategy is that it limits your downside loss possibility to the amount you paid for the put inclusive of commissions and the commission cost to buy the stock and later sell it through the exercise of the put. Although this loss-limiting type of adventure may have attraction for some investors and proponents, the drawbacks of the strategy are much too great for me to recommend the strategy to the conservative investor.

The advocates of married puts point out the following two attractive features:

- The upside profit potential in the insured stock position is unrestricted and unlimited during the life of the put.
- The downside risk of stock ownership is absolutely known in advance, is finite, and is limited to a precise, calculable amount during the life of the put.

To the investor in common stocks who is uninitiated in options and who may at one time or another have experienced stock price drops of great magnitude in one or more of the portfolio stocks owned, the married put strategy can appear to be heaven sent.

There is an old expression that goes, "Appearances are often deceiving." And, to me, so it is with married puts.

To help you better understand my aversion to the married put strategy, I will walk you through an illustrative example, pointing out a more viable and less risky alternative strategy to the married put.

Let's assume that you have done your homework. You have spotted an interesting common stock, obtained and reviewed the latest available annual and quarterly reports, and read the Standard & Poor's sheet as well as all available research put out by recognized, able departments of well-established brokerage firms. Before making a financial commitment to the stock of your choice, you get option quotations on it. The option quotes with XYZ at 30 in late March are as follows:

	Strike Price	Option Price	Expiration Month
Call Options	30	2	June
Put Options	30	2	June

Your contemplated purchase is for 1,000 shares of XYZ at 30.

If you decide to accept the married put strategy, you will buy 1,000 XYZ at 30 and simultaneously buy 10 June 30 puts at 2 each. You identify the put as a hedge, thereby increasing your cost basis in XYZ by the total amount paid for the put insurance.

Example 1: Married Put Strategy Stock Purchase and Put Purchase

Stock XYZ is at 30; XYZ June 30 puts are at 2.

In Late March		At June Expiration, XYZ is below 30	
Buy 1,000 @ 30	$30,000	1,000 XYZ sold by put	
Plus full-service commission	+495	exercise @ 30	$30,000
Net stock cost	$30,495	Less full-service commission	−495
		Net proceeds	$29,505
Buy 10 XYZ June 30 puts @ 2	$ 2,000		
Plus full-service commission	+130	Net loss on exercise of put	
Total cost of married put	$32,625	($32,625 − $29,505)	($3,120)

Following are the results you would have at various possible prices of XYZ at the June expiration. All results shown are inclusive of commissions at full-service prices.

June Expiration Possible XYZ Price	Result
Below 30	($3,120)
40	6,815
50	16,755
60	26,695

You would need for XYZ to be at $33^1/8$ at June expiration to break even, assuming that you sell the stock at that price.

If you use the married put strategy, you are always forced into incurring the cost of the put insurance and the cost of stock commission expenses to buy and later to sell the stock.

Furthermore, if you use the married put, you will often be on the horns of an investment dilemma at put expiration time when your insured stock is just at or above the put exercise price.

If you really like a stock and its price potential by put expiration time and XYZ is just at or above the put exercise price, you must do one of the following:

- Buy new put insurance for another period.
- Decide to own the stock uninsured with substantial exposure to risk of a stock price drop should your judgment prove wrong.
- Bear the loss of the cost of the initial put insurance.

Once you get caught up in the put insurance strategy, you could find out that the high cost of that insurance through your continued purchase of protective puts approximates the put exercise price at each successive expiration. An option strategy that is better and more viable than the married put is the simple outright purchase of call options on your chosen stock.

The advantages of long call options versus married puts are the following:

- Avoidance of stock commission expenses to buy and to sell stock.
- The money not used to buy the stock normally would earn money market fund interest greater than the typical cash dividends paid by common stocks deemed risky enough to warrant a protective put purchase.

With long call options you have the following advantages:

- Predetermined risk just as has the user of married puts.
- Unlimited upside potential just as has the user of married puts.
- Tax deductibility of any losses sustained.

Now, let's examine the viable alternative to a married put, which is the very simple outright purchase of a call option.

Example 2: Call Purchase as Substitute for Married Put

Stock XYZ is at 30; XYZ June 30 calls are at 2.

In Late March		At June Expiration XYZ is below 30	
Buy 10 XYZ June calls @ 2	$2,000	10 XYZ June 30 calls expire	
Plus full-service commission	+130	worthless	
Net call cost	$2,130	Net loss	($2,130)

The $30,495 not used to buy 1,000 XYZ at 30 (see Example 1) is invested in a money market fund.

Following are the results at various possible prices of XYZ at the June expiration. All results shown are inclusive of commissions at full-service prices.

June Expiration Possible XYZ Price	Result
Below 30	($2,130)
40	7,648
50	17,530
60	27,295

When you compare the possible results of a married put versus a long call, it should become quite apparent that for every possible price of XYZ at the June expiration, the long call strategy is superior. If you hold a long call instead of a married put, you are likely to lose less, make more, and break even at a lower price level.

When you add to those advantages the interest being earned by the money invested in the money market fund (interest that is greater than the typical cash dividends paid to holders of married puts), you may be inclined to accept my favoring call buying over married puts.

Some of you may still be wondering why many brokerage firms so actively promote the married put strategy. Let me help you look at the two strategies through the eyes of the brokerage firms:

- Buy stock–buy put creates substantial stock commissions that are shared by the firm and the soliciting broker.
- Buy stock–buy put can be certain to place a limit on loss during the put life.
- Buy stock–buy put seldom leads to lawsuits or customer complaints because of the insurance aspect of the strategy.
- Buy stock–buy put has gained wide acceptance as a type of conservative option strategy akin to covered call writing.
- Long call purchases are viewed almost universally as outright speculations.
- Investors who lose on long calls are more likely to prevail in a dispute that goes to court or to arbitration.
- Long calls as a substitute for married puts might be deemed an unsuitable activity for investors who could easily obtain approval to execute married puts.

Despite all the foregoing, a careful mathematical analysis of the two strategies should heavily favor the purchase of long calls instead of committing to married puts.

When you choose the long call strategy over the married put strategy, you should be disciplined enough to maintain in reserve the funds you do not use to buy the stock. Should the long calls die worthless, you will then be in a position to make a decision to buy the originally contemplated share amount with the reserve funds or to buy new long calls at the same or lower strike.

You must realize that the option market is volatile and that option premiums vary considerably based on whether investors are optimistic or pessimistic about future rises in stock prices. When investors are extremely negative, or bearish, about the outlook for increases in common stock prices, put option premiums tend to equal or exceed call option premiums:

- For the same underlying stock.
- At the same strike price.
- For the same expiration month.

When investors are extremely positive, or bullish, about the outlook for increases in common stock prices, the premiums for call options tend to exceed those for put options:

- For the same underlying stock.
- At the same strike price.
- For the same expiration month.

Investors substituting long call positions for married put positions can afford to pay more for the long call than the married put investor pays for the put and still have a more viable strategy.

Despite my bias against the normal married put strategy advocated by many brokerage firms, there is a particular circumstance in which married puts may be a very viable strategy. This special circumstance comes about when in-the-money puts are available under the following three conditions:

1. With very little time premiums over the intrinsic worth.
2. With a narrow distance from a market price to put price (15% or less).
3. With sufficient time to put expiration to accommodate a stock price rise (more than 30 days).

In addition to the preceding, your chance for success using married puts would be substantially increased by any substantial commission discounts you can get.

The following example might help clarify the one possible viable use of married puts. Assume that XYZ is 27¼ and that XYZ puts are available as follows in late March:

Strike Price	April Call Price	July Call Price
30	3	June

The investor in married puts normally has two objectives in mind in undertaking the married put strategy: (1) containing risk to a low predeterminable amount and (2) participating in an unlimited price rise in XYZ during the life of the put.

Example 3: Married Put Stock Purchase and Put Purchase

Stock XYZ is at 27¼; XYZ June 30 puts are at 3.

In Late March		At June Expiration XYZ is below 30	
Buy 1,000 XYZ @ 27¼	$27,250	Sell 1,000 XYZ by put	
Plus full-service commission	+470	exercise @ 30	$30,000
Net stock cost	$27,720	Less full-service commission	−445
		Net proceeds	$29,505
Buy 10 XYZ June 30 puts @ 3	$ 3,000		
Plus full-service commission	+142	Net loss on put exercise	($1,357)
Net put purchase cost	$ 3,142		
Total cost of married put	$30,862		

In the foregoing example, the worst-case scenario would show a loss of $1,357 at full-service commissions. If commission discounts were obtained, the loss would be substantially less and further reduced by any cash dividends received.

You would need a stock price rise of approximately 15% to reach a breakeven point. A price rise greater than 15% before the expiration of the put would place you in a profit position.

Following are the results when you invest in married puts, using in-the-money puts, at various possible prices of XYZ at the June expiration. All results shown are inclusive of all commissions at full-service prices.

June Expiration Possible XYZ Price	Result
Below 30	($1,357)
40	8,588
50	18,518
60	28,458

In another scenario, if you invest in in-the-money married puts, you may be able to completely or partially eliminate risk at the time of the execution of the married put (or shortly thereafter) by issuing calls with a higher strike price than the price of the in-the-money puts owned as protection for the stock. The out-of-the-money call premium you collect may be sufficient to eliminate partially or completely the projected loss on a put exercise. Issuing the calls while decreasing the risk of an overall loss puts a possible lid on profits should the calls be exercised.

The variations and possible outcomes can be almost mind-boggling, but the bottom line is that if the married put strategy contains in-the-money puts with little time premium, the strategy becomes a low-cost way to seek large profits.

CHAPTER 22

Speculative Purchases of Put and Call Options

Of all the possible strategies offered by the stock option world, perhaps none is so exciting and attractive as the outright purchase of call options. Investors worldwide have been drawn to purchasing call options as if a high-powered magnet with a strong pulling power was being focused on a portion of their financial assets.

FEATURES OF LONG CALL OPTIONS

The powerful, attractive features of call option purchases have made them the overwhelmingly favorite strategy of option buyers everywhere. Let's briefly review the features that have long made the call option the favorite tool of speculators.

Simplicity

Call option purchases are more easily understood by investors than any other option strategy. That understanding, in part, may come from the real estate world where deposits (down payments—in effect, option money) are used to tie up a piece of real estate at an established price until a closing takes place. The down payment, or option money, serves as a forfeiture should no closing take place.

Leverage

Investors are drawn to call option buying by the very high degree of leverage that is obtainable. Hundreds of dollars invested in long call options can control, for a period, underlying stock that is valued in the thousands.

Limited Risk

Speculators who buy call options particularly like the fact that their risk is absolutely limited to the amount they pay for their call options. Owners of call options never get asked for margin, nor are they required to put up any additional funds regardless of how low the underlying stock declines during the life of their call options.

Although buyers of call options do run the risk of total loss of the funds invested in calls, their venture is not just a win-or-lose proposition. Buyers of calls may experience any one of several possible outcomes as a result of their speculation, such as:

- Lose all.
- Lose part.
- Break even.
- Win a little.
- Win a lot.

Unlimited Profit Potential

Call option buyers have no ceiling placed on what they might possibly earn as a result of their call option speculation. Their losses are fixed, but their profit possibilities are without restriction. This feature probably exerts the strongest pull on speculators of any of the attractive features associated with call buying. The dream of the big win as a result of call buying activity makes many an investor's mouth water enough to accept the risk of 100% loss of the funds invested in the purchase of call options.

Tax Deductibility of Losses

Buyers of call options should certainly be alert and aware that any money spent for the purchase of call options is subject to total loss. However, even if a total loss is encountered from a venture into long calls, the option loss is diminished by the regulations of the Internal Revenue Service (IRS).

The IRS allows losses from call option purchases to be used without limit to offset any capital gains earned! If no capital gains exist for offset by losses, you are allowed to deduct up to $3,000 in a single tax year from your highest taxed income from losses sustained from long calls bought.

Any call buying losses that are not used up as offsets for realized gains or as deductions from highest taxed income may be carried forward indefinitely to future years until used up as deductions or as offsets to gains.

Time

Purchasers of long calls acquire a block of time during which their hope of profit may be realized. The period purchased may vary from as little as one day to as long as nine months. The bulk of long calls purchased, however, usually have terms of one to three months in which an investor's expectations for a price rise in the shares underlying the long calls may be met. To have the time to root for a winner and time to change one's mind and get out of the long call position (at a profit or a loss) is a great attraction for speculators.

Now let's take a close look at some possible results you may obtain if you are willing to risk total loss of approximately $5,000 through an investment in long call options. Tables 22.1, 22.2, and 22.3 depict the various possible outcomes of your speculation were you to make each of the three following investments:

1. Invest approximately $5,000 in XYZ July 50 in-the-money calls.
2. Invest approximately $5,000 in XYZ July 55 at-the-money calls.
3. Invest approximately $5,000 in XYZ July 60 out-of-the-money calls.

In Table 22.1, you:

-   Control 800 shares of XYZ.
-   Break even if XYZ at the July expiration is 56³/₈.

Table 22.1   Purchase of In-the-Money Calls[a]

At Expiration Possible XYZ Price	Call Option Cost with Commission	Proceeds of Option Sale Less Commission	Net Profit or (Loss)
Below 50	$4,950	$ 0	($4,950)
55	4,950	3,860	($1,090)
60	4,950	7,815	2,865
65	4,950	11,770	6,820
70	4,950	15,725	10,775

[a]In late March the XYZ market price is 55. You buy 8 July 50 calls at 6 each.

Table 22.2   Purchase of At-the-Money Calls[a]

At Expiration Possible XYZ Price	Call Option Cost with Commission	Proceeds of Option Sale Less Commission	Net Profit or (Loss)
Below 55	$4,975	$ 0	($ 4,975)
60	4,975	5,820	845
65	4,975	11,730	6,755
70	4,975	17,670	12,695
75	4,975	23,600	18,625

[a]In late March the XYZ market price is 55. You buy 12 July 55 calls at 4 each.

- Will profit $800 for each point XYZ has risen over 56% by the July expiration.
- Will lose only part of your investment if at the July expiration XYZ is over 50 and under 56$3/8$.

In Table 22.2, you:

- Control 1,200 shares of XYZ.
- Break even if XYZ at the July expiration is 59$3/8$.
- Will profit $1,200 for each point XYZ has risen over 59$3/8$ by the July expiration.
- Will lose only part of your investment if at the July expiration XYZ is over 55 and under 59$3/8$.

Table 22.3   Purchase of Out-of-the-Money Calls[a]

At Expiration Possible XYZ Price	Call Option Cost with Commission	Proceeds of Option Sale Less Commission	Net Profit or (Loss)
Below 60	$5,090	$ 0	($ 5,090)
65	5,090	15,585	10,495
70	5,090	31,435	26,345
75	5,090	47,300	42,210

[a]In late March the XYZ market price is 55. You buy 32 July 60s at 1$1/2$ each.

Now let's take a careful look at Table 22.3, the third and last table in this series.

In Table 22.3, you:

- Control 3,200 shares of XYZ.
- Break even if XYZ at the July expiration is 61$3/4$.
- Will profit $3,200 for each point XYZ has risen over 61$3/4$ by the July expiration.
- Will lose only part of your investment if at the July expiration XYZ is over 60 and under 61$3/4$.

In examining the three tables, notice that with relatively equal sums invested in long calls:

- The higher the strike price is, the greater is your leverage in terms of shares under control.
- The lower the strike price is, the lower is the price of the underlying stock you need to reach the break even point at expiration.

Table 22.4 briefly recaps the preceding three tables so that you can more readily comprehend the differences in outcomes that result from your selection of strike price, even when you invest similar amounts.

Table 22.4   Recap of Procedures

	Amount Invested	Breakeven Point at Expiration	Shares under Option	Profit at 65	Profit at 70
XYZ 50 Table 22.1 In-the-Money	$4,950	56$3/8$	800	$ 2,865	$10,775
XYZ 55 Table 22.2 At-the-Money	4,975	59$3/8$	1,200	6,755	12,695
XYZ 60 Table 22.3 Out-of-the-Money	5,090	6$3/4$	3,200	10,495	26,345

GUIDELINES FOR BUYING LONG CALL OPTIONS

If you do get the burning desire to speculate through the purchase of long call options, you may want to adhere to some of my guidelines for that strategy.

Never Overcommit

No matter how confident you are of an expected rise in shares underlying a call purchase, do not buy calls beyond an amount that you feel you could well afford to lose.

Buy Enough Time

Whatever your expectation of a coming upward price move in a selected stock, be careful to select an expiration month from those available that is beyond the time in which you expect the price move to occur. Nothing is more disheartening to the buyer of a call option than to have call options expire just before a big upmove in the underlying stock occurs.

Control Greed

If profits are quickly available from a call option purchase, consider cashing in part of the holdings so as to recover most or all of the total that you have risked. You can then keep the balance of the calls you hold in the hope of reaping a huge gain.

Choose the Strike Price Carefully

Select a strike price close to the market price of the underlying stock. This sacrifice of some upside leverage allows for partial or total recovery of the amount risked in the call purchase on just a small percentage rise in the underlying stock. Plenty of profit potential exists if a large percentage rise occurs in the underlying stock.

Research the Stock Underlying the Call Purchase

Thoroughly review the fundamentals that tend to influence a stock's upmove, such as the following:

- Large boost in dividend.
- Large increase in earnings per share.
- A new invention or a discovery of magnitude.
- Undervalued assets that could attract takeover interest.

Speculative put purchases have most of the same attractive features as for call purchases, such as:

- High degree of leverage.
- High profit potential.
- Limited and predeterminable risk.
- Tax deductibility of any losses sustained.

The two main differences between put purchase speculation and call purchase speculation are:

1. Put purchasers seek profits from a downmove in a stock's price.
2. The profit potential in a put purchase is always limited by zero in the stock price.

The same guidelines that I have suggested for speculative purchases of calls apply to speculative purchases of puts.

Conservative investors may occasionally take a fling buying puts or calls to test their judgment of a particular stock's future price movement. Right judgments usually foster additional flings in option purchasing. Take great care never to risk more than you can easily afford as a loss.

WARNING

Regular and consistent purchasing of puts and calls is best left to professional traders who operate with little commission expenses and who are constantly willing to jeopardize their capital while searching for large gains.

Buying puts and calls is simply not for the following:

- The faint of heart.
- Those investors living on a fixed income where losses would hurt their lifestyle.
- The investor who is uninformed and uneducated about option usage and risks.

CHAPTER **23**

The Diagonal Call Option Spread

One of the most interesting and intriguing of call option spread strategies lies in executing diagonal spreads with call options. In this particular strategy, you enter into the speculative venture through the following:

- Purchases of far-month calls.
- Sales of near-month calls with quantities sold equal to or less than quantities bought.
- Obtaining a strike price in the far-month calls that is lower than the strike price in the near-month calls that are issued.

In undertaking this adventure in the option world, you hope for a price rise in the underlying stock before the expiration of the far-month calls that you own and after the expiration of the near-month calls you sell short.

When you execute diagonal call option spreads, you have to realize that your expectation of a rising price in the underlying stock:

- May never occur.
- May occur during the life of the short call obligation.
- May occur after the expiration of the short call obligation and before the expiration of the long call position.

You must also accept the following:

- Profit potential is limited until the near-month obligation is extinguished through purchase or expiration.

- Profit potential is unlimited after the near-month obligation has been eliminated and before the expiration of far-month calls that you hold.

Because of fear that their judgment of a coming price rise in the underlying stock may be wrong, investors buying the long far-month call options often seek to lessen the risk of the purchase of the far-month calls through collecting premiums from the sale of near-month calls with a higher strike price than those bought.

Many of the more astute, informed option traders believe that the greatest overvalue in call option premiums exists in out-of-the-money calls for near expiration months. These marketwise diagonal call option spreaders simply make an attempt to capture this overvalue.

In the diagonal call option spreader's dream world:

- The near-month short call obligation will expire unexercised.
- After the expiration of the short call obligation, the underlying stock will rise substantially before the expiration of the long calls. The long call position then offers unlimited appreciation possibilities.

In executing diagonal call option spreads, there are many possible outcomes. To help educate you without your being overwhelmed, I am just going to review a few of the more frequently occurring outcomes.

Let's assume that you have selected an underlying stock that shows the potential for a substantial price rise. You are willing to accept the risk of 100% loss of any funds you commit to the purchase of long calls on the selected stock, reduced by the amount collected from the sale of near-month calls with a higher strike price.

You carefully review the option prices for the chosen stock. Stock XYZ's current price is 25. In late March, the XYZ call options are available as follows:

| | *Expiration Months* | |
Strike Price	May Option	August Price
25	2	3
30	3/4	1 1/4

You decide to establish a diagonal call option spread position, selling call options in quantities that equal the call option quantities you buy. You establish a margin account and deposit sufficient collateral to meet the firm's minimum requirements. Notice that a long call serves as approved collateral for a short call as long as (1) the expiration date in the long call is more distant than the short call, and (2) the strike price in the long call is the same as or higher than in the short call.

Example 1: First Possible Outcome

In Late March		At May Expiration XYZ is below 25	At August Expiration XYZ is below 25
Buy 10 XYZ Aug 25s @ 3	$3,000	10 short XYZ May 30s expire worthless	10 long XYZ Aug 25s expire worthless
Plus full-service commission	+142		
Net cost	$3,142	Investor nets $665	Investor loses $3,142
Sell 10 XYZ May 30s @ 3/4	$ 750		
Less full-service commission	−85		
Net proceeds	$ 665		
After applying net proceeds to net cost of calls bought, the investor's net out-of-pocket invested in the 10 diagonal call option spreads is $2,477 ($3,142−$665).		Net loss on combined transaction is $2,447 (inclusive of commission).	

Example 1 shows the worst possible outcome for the diagonal call option spreader.

Using the same set of facts for the initial stock price, strike price, and expiration months, let's look at Example 2.

In Example 2, XYZ rises substantially over the strike price in the near-term May short calls. You always run the risk of the short call position of the diagonal call option spread being exercised.

Example 2: Second Possible Outcome

In Late March		At May Expiration XYZ is 35	
Buy 10 XYZ Aug 25s @ 3	$3,000	Buy 10 May 30s @ 5	$ 5,000
Plus full-service commission	+142	Plus full-service commission	+165
Net purchase cost	$3,142	Net purchase cost	$ 5,165
Sell 10 XYZ May 30s @ 3/4	$ 750	Sell 10 Aug 25s @ 10	$10,000
Less full-service commission	−85	Less full-service commission	−225
Net proceeds	$ 665	Net proceeds	$ 9,775
Net out-of-pocket invested in the 10 diagonal spreads ($3,142 − $665)	$2,477	Net excess of sales over purchases	$ 4,610
		Less out-of-pocket spread entry cost	−2,477
		Net profit (inclusive of commissions)	$ 2,133

When you deal in diagonal call option spreads, you must always carefully watch any stock price runups above the short call exercise price. Should the short call go deep in the money and trade with little time premium over the intrinsic worth, you should close out the diagonal call option spread to prevent incurring stock commission expenses to buy and to sell the underlying shares.

Now let's take a look at a dream outcome for a diagonal call option spread investor, again using the same expiration months, strike prices, and option prices (see Example 3).

In Example 3, you experienced the best of both worlds:

- XYZ stayed below the near month (May) strike of 30 so that the entire net premium initially received was earned.
- After the short May 30 calls expired, XYZ rose to where the long Aug 25s could be sold at the August expiration for their intrinsic worth of $1,000 per call option.

Now look at Example 4 for another possible outcome for an investor in diagonal call options. Once more, the expiration months, strike prices, and option prices in the initial establishment of the call option diagonal spread are the same as in the other three examples.

Example 3: Third Possible Outcome

In Late March	At May Expiration XYZ is under 30	At August Expiration XYZ is 35
Buy 10 XYZ Aug 25s @ 3 $3,000	10 XYZ May 30s expire worthless	10 XYZ 25s sold for 10 $10,000
Plus full-service commission +142		Less full-service commission −225
Net purchase cost $3,142		Net sale proceeds $ 9,775
Sell 10 XYZ May 30s @ 3/4 $ 750	Investor nets $665	Less out-of-pocket spread entry cost −2,477
Less full-service commission −85		Net profit on
Net proceeds $ 665		10 Aug 25s $ 7,298
Net out-of-pocket invested in the 10 diagonal call option spreads ($3,142 − $665) $2,477	Total $7,298 Net profit +665 from closing both call option positions (commissions included) $7,963	

In Example 4, XYZ rose to 30 at the near month May expiration. The 10 XYZ May 30s originally issued for 3/4 each expired unexercised, allowing you to net the premium originally received. With XYZ at 30 at the May expiration and the May 30s expired, you could either (1) hold the long Aug 25s hoping for a continued price rise in XYZ as shown in Example 3, or (2) reduce your out-of-pocket risk of $2,477 in 10 long Aug 25s by issuing 10 short Aug 30s.

In Example 4, the assumption is made that in May with XYZ at 30, call options at 30 with three months' life could be issued for 2 1/2 each. Collecting the second premium for issuing short XYZ call options lowers your risk to only $112, inclusive of commissions at full-service prices.

You should also notice that the second call issuance backed by the ownership of the 10 Aug 25s changes the spread to a bullish perpendicular call option spread that is characterized by the following:

- Short call options backed by long call options.
- Same expiration month.

Example 4: Fourth Possible Outcome

In Late March		At May Expiration XYZ is 30		At August Expiration XYZ is 35	
Buy 10 XYZ Aug 25s @ 3	$3,000	10 XYZ May 30s expire worthless		10 XYZ Aug 25s sold for 10	$10,000
Plus full-service commission	+142	Investor nets	$ 665	Less full-service commission	−225
Net purchase cost	$3,142			Net sale proceeds	$ 9,775
Sell 10 XYZ May 30s @ 3/4	$ 750			10 XYZ Aug 30s bought @ 5	$ 5,000
Less full-service commission	−85	10 XYZ Aug 30s sold for 2 1/2	$2,500	Plus full-service commission	+165
Net proceeds	$ 665	Less full-service commission	−135	Net purchase cost	$ 5,165
		Net proceeds	$2,365		
Net out-of-pocket invested in 10 diagonal call option spreads	$2,477			Net excess of sales over purchases	$ 4,610
		Initial out-of-pocket spread cost	$2,477	Less out-of-pocket spreads cost	−112
		Less net proceeds of Aug 30s sold	−2,365		
				Net profit (inclusive of commissions)	$ 4,498
		Net out-of-pocket left invested in the 10 diagonal call option spreads	$ 112		

- Strike price in short calls higher than strike price in the long calls.
- Quantities same for both positions.

To sum up, the diagonal call option spread strategy should be used only by option market sophisticates. Conservative investors would be well advised to avoid this very complicated investment technique except, perhaps, to gain option market experience firsthand by doing and to test their judgment of a particular stock's future price movement.

If you are contemplating testing the diagonal call option spread strategies, you should understand that if you purchase the most distant call option, you may have to issue an intermediate-month call with a higher strike price rather than the nearest month call with a higher strike price. You may have to use this strategy alternative because:

- The required or wanted strike price in the nearest month call may not be available for trading.
- The premium relationship between the nearest month call and the intermediate-month call favors the issuance of the intermediate-month call.

In all the preceding examples, the assumption was that both sides of the diagonal call option spread were executed simultaneously. In the real option world, the simultaneous execution of both the long and the short call portions of the diagonal call option spread is the most usual method of entering into the strategy. There is, however, another method of entering into a diagonal call option spread position that is used fairly often. This method is called *legging*. In legging, you initially position only one side of the intended diagonal call option spread position. You establish the other leg at a later time at a more advantageous price should your judgment prove correct.

The trouble with legging is that while you are searching for a better reward potential, you expose yourself to substantially greater risk. Legging into a diagonal call option spread by first issuing the short calls exposes you to unlimited risk and should absolutely be avoided! Legging into a diagonal call option spread by first purchasing the long calls limits your risk exactly to the next amount paid for the long calls.

As a long call legger, you hope for a stock price rise (after you establish the long call position) that will be large enough to enable you to sell the short call portion of the diagonal call option spread for possibly as much as you paid for the long calls. If this happy circumstance occurs, one or more of the following could happen:

- You could recover the amount you paid for the long calls from the premiums you collected from the sale of the short calls.
- You could reduce your risk to zero, or even lock in a profit.
- You could retain the possibility of an unlimited profit potential.

Example 5: Legged Diagonal Call Option Spread Strategy

Let's take a look at a legged entry into a diagonal call option spread position. Again, use the figures from our previous four examples. The current price of XYZ is 25. In late March, XYZ call options are available as shown below:

	Expiration Months	
Strike Price	May Option	August Price
25	2	3
30	$3/4$	$1^1/4$

Table 23.1

Leg 1: In Late March XYZ is 25		Leg 2: In April XYZ is 33		At May Expiration XYZ is 35	
Buy 10 XYZ Aug 25s @ 3	$3,000	Sell 10 XYZ May 30s @ 3½	$3,500	Buy 10 XYZ May 30s @ 5	$ 5,000
Plus full-service commission	+142	Less full-service commission	−150	Plus full-service commission	+165
Net purchase cost	$3,142	Net proceeds	$3,350	Net purchase cost	$ 5,165
				Sell 10 XYZ Aug 25s @ 10	$10,000
				Less full-service commission	−225
				Net proceeds	$ 9,775
				Net excess of sales over purchases	$ 4,610
				Plus excess of April sales over March cost	+208
				Net profit (inclusive of commissions)	$ 4,818

In the expectation of a near-term price rise in XYZ, you leg into an anticipated diagonal call option spread position through purchasing 10 XYZ Aug 25s at 3 each. In April XYZ surges to 33, and in May XYZ 30s rise to $3^1/2$. You sell 10 XYZ May 30s for $3^1/2$ each. Some possible outcomes of the legged-in positions are shown in Table 23.1.

In Example 5, you risked total loss of the purchase cost of 10 Aug 25s of $3,142 in the first established leg of your planned diagonal call option spread. Luckily, XYZ advanced from 25 to 33 shortly after your long call purchase. With the stock at 33, May expiration in-the-money calls at 30 were available to be issued for $3^1/2$.

Selling 10 May calls at $3^1/2$ each enabled you to eliminate completely all risk of loss in the ownership of 10 Aug 25s and provided a guaranteed minimum profit of $208.

Selling the 10 May 30s at $3^1/2$ each placed you in the happy position of:

- Earning over $4,800 if XYZ remained over 30 until the May expiration.
- Earning $208 if XYZ collapsed and remained below 25 through the August expiration.
- Earning an unlimited amount if XYZ fell below 30 by the May expiration and rose above 25 by the August expiration by an unceilinged amount.

CHAPTER 24

The Bullish Perpendicular Call Option Spread

The bullish perpendicular call option spread strategy is certainly quite a mouthful of option-world words that are used to describe a very popular and frequently used strategy.

Participants in the option world also refer to this strategy by other descriptive terms, such as *vertical bull call spread* and *bullish call price spread*. Whatever the label ascribed to the strategy, the strategy involves the investor in establishing a long call option position and a short call option position. Basic characteristics of the strategy are the following:

- The expiration month in both the long and the short call positions is the same.

- The strike price in the long call position is lower than the strike price in the short call position.

- The quantities of short calls sold equal the quantities of long calls bought.

- The stock underlying the short and the long calls is the same.

One of the driving forces that leads speculators to seek profits through bullish perpendicular call option spreads is obtaining a call on a chosen stock at an out-of-pocket cost that is substantially less than the going market cost of the long call portion of the spread.

If you establish a bullish perpendicular call option spread, you can immediately apply all the net proceeds you receive from the sale of the high strike price calls to the reduction of the amount needed to purchase the long low strike price calls. This is permitted by option margin rules, and it is the way your lower out-of-pocket cost comes about.

Other facts that you should make indelible in your memory are the following:

- Bullish call option spreading is speculation—a risky venture.
- Bullish call option spreading can be done only in a margin account.
- Bullish call option spreading entails the deposit of some minimum collateral (the amount varies among firms from $2,000 and up) in addition to any out-of-pocket spread difference required.

When you invest in bullish call option spreads, you severely restrict profit potential in return for obtaining bargain-priced long calls. Is the trade-off worthwhile? Perhaps you will be able to judge the trade-off value more accurately after reviewing the following three examples. And just maybe you will come to share my view that in most instances surrendering un-limited profit potential for a cost reduction in long calls isn't such a good deal.

Example 1: Long Call in the Money

Assume that XYZ's current market price is 26$^{1}/_{2}$. You like the potential for a future price rise in XYZ, and you want to participate in a way that will reduce risk. You obtain call option quotes for XYZ in early April, as follows:

Strike Price	Call Option Price	Expiration Month
30	$^{3}/_{4}$	July
25	2$^{3}/_{4}$	July

The maximum profit potential occurs if XYZ is at 30 at the July expiration and if the July 30s expire unexercised. The profit is a result of:

- A 117.3% return on the out-of-pocket risk capital invested.
- A 117.3% return earned on a 13.2% rise in the price of the underlying stock over its price at the time the spread was established.

In Early April XYZ is 26¹/₂		*At July Expiration XYZ is 30*	
Buy 10 XYZ July 25 calls @ 2³/₄	$2,750	10 short XYZ July 30s expire worthless	
Plus full-service commission	+140	Sell 10 long XYZ July 25s @ 5	$5,000
Net purchase cost	$2,890	Less full-service commission	−165
		Net sale proceeds	$4,835
Sell 10 XYZ July 30s @ ³/₄	$ 750	Net out-of-pocket cost	−2,225
Less full-service commission	−85	Net profit (inclusive of commissions)	$2,610
Net sale proceeds	$ 665		
Net out-of-pocket cost ($2,890 − $665)	$2,225		

Other outcomes for the bullish perpendicular call option spread shown in Example 1 at various other possible prices of XYZ at the July expiration are as in Table 24.1.

As you can see from Table 24.1, no matter how high XYZ rises above 30, your profit is limited. The profit declines after 30 as a result of commissions. The investor will break even at the July expiration if XYZ has advanced from the 26¹/₂ price at the time you initiated the spread to 27¹/₂, a gain of 1 point, or 3.8%. No matter how low XYZ declines below 25, your loss is fixed and is limited to your out-of-pocket spread entry cost of $2,225.

Now let's take a look at another example of a bullish perpendicular call option spread. The circumstances used in Example 2 are different from those in Example 1 in that the spread features:

- A higher priced stock.
- A long out-of-the-money call as the hedge for the short call obligation.

Table 24.1

Possible Price of XYZ at July Expiration	Out-of-Pocket Spread Entry Cost[a]	Profit or (Loss) on Spread Liquidation[a]
Below 25	$2,225	($2,225)
27	2,225	(350)
32	2,225	2,495
37	2,225	2,375

[a]Including commissions.

Example 2: Long Call out of the Money

Assume that XYZ's market price is 39. You have researched XYZ, and you have arrived at the conclusion that the share price may rise during the next few months. The shares are highly volatile, so you decide to make a defined and limited risk investment in XYZ through establishing a bullish perpendicular call option spread. The call option quotations for XYZ in early April are as follows:

Strike Price	Call Option Price	Expiration Month
45	2	July
40	3¹/₂	July

In Early April XYZ is 39		At July Expiration XYZ is 45	
Buy 10 XYZ July 40s @ 3¹/₂	$3,500	10 short XYZ July 45s expire worthless	
Plus full-service commission	+150		
Net purchase cost	$3,650	Sell 10 long XYZ 40s @ 5	$5,000
		Less full-service commission	−165
Sell 10 XYZ July 45s @ 2	$2,000	Net sale proceeds	$4,835
Less-full-service commission	−125	Net out-of-pocket cost	−1,775
Net sales proceeds	$1,875	Net profit (including commissions)	$3,060
Net out-of-pocket cost ($3,650−$1,875)	$1,775		

Your maximum profit potential occurs if XYZ is 45 at the July expiration and if the July 45s expire unexercised. The profit earned represented the following:

- A 172.6% return on the out-of-pocket risk capital invested in the spread.
- A 172.6% return earned on a 15.3% rise in the underlying stock from the price prevailing at the time the spread was established.

That magnificent mouthwatering maximum return of 172.6% (unannualized) is just the type of possibility that entices investors into testing the strategy on a selected stock. Other possible outcomes for the bullish perpendicular call option spread illustrated in Example 2 at various prices of XYZ are shown in Table 24.2

As can be seen in Table 24.2, no matter how high XYZ rises above 45, your profit is limited. The profit decline after a price rise over 45 is a result of the impact of commission costs to liquidate the spread. In the situation illustrated in Example 2, you will break even at the July expiration if XYZ has advanced from 39 (its cost when you initiated the spread) to 42$\frac{1}{8}$, representing a gain of 3$\frac{1}{8}$ points, or 8%.

No matter how low XYZ shares might sink below 40, your loss is fixed and limited to your out-of-pocket cost of entering the spread, $1,775.

Many experienced option traders try to leg into a bullish perpendicular call option spread position. They start out with a purchase of long calls. Their hope is that after the long call purchase is made, a rise in the underlying shares will take place, which would enable them to issue short calls at a higher strike and for a greater dollar amount than could have been collected at the time of their long call purchase.

Example 3: Spread Established by Legging

Example 3 depicts a leg-in entry into a bullish perpendicular call option spread position.

Your maximum profit potential (after issuing the 10 July 30s at 2) occurs if XYZ at the July expiration is 30 and if the July 30s expire unexercised. By legging into the spread, you reduced your maximum loss potential to $1,015. The profit earned at the maximum profit point represented the following:

- A 132% return on the original capital invested in the long call position.

- A 260% return on the out-of-pocket capital at risk when the July 30 short calls were issued.

Table 24.2

Possible Price of XYZ at July Expiration	Out-of-Pocket Spread Entry Cost[a]	Profit or (Loss) on Spread Liquidation[a]
Below 40	$1,775	($1,775)
42	1,775	100
47	1,775	2,910
52	1,775	2,825

[a]Including commissions.

In Early April *XYZ is 26 1/2*		*In Late April* *XYZ is 29*		*In July* *XYZ is 30*	
Buy 10 XYZ July		Sell 10 XYZ July		10 short XYZ July 30s	
25s @ 2 3/4	$2,750	30s @ 2	$2,000	expire worthless	
Plus full-service		Less full-service			
commission	+140	commission	−125	Sell 10 long XYZ	
Net purchase cost	$2,890	Net proceeds	$1,875	July 25s @ 5	$5,000
		Net out-of-pocket cost		Less full-service	
		($2,890–$1,875)	$1,015	commission	−165
				Net sale proceeds	$4,835
				Net out-of-pocket cost	−1,015
				Net profit (inclusive of commissions)	$3,820

Having come this far, you should be able to perceive certain special aspects of bullish perpendicular call option spreads, which are as follows:

- Limited and precisely definable risks.
- Restricted profit potential.
- High degree of leverage.
- Relatively low percentage of change in stock price needed to reach a breakeven point.
- Relatively low percentage of change in stock price needed to earn very high rates of return on the risk capital.

Most *conservative* investors do not execute bullish perpendicular call option spreads. Those who want to attempt it should do so only on rare occasions when the following conditions are met:

- They have a decided opinion about an upcoming price rise in the underlying stock.
- They have decided to take a fling with a modest amount of capital, the loss of which would not be material to their asset structure or emotionally upsetting.
- They have thoroughly investigated and gained understanding of the strategy.

GUIDELINES

Those speculative investors who wish to partake of the strategy more frequently would do well to adhere to some of my guidelines that follow.

Aim for Large Percentage Gains

Select only those bullish perpendicular call option spread opportunities in which the out-of-pocket cash outlay can at least be doubled after commission expenses if the underlying stock were to rise to or beyond the high strike price by the expiration date.

Seek Profits from Less than a 15% Move to High Strike

Enter into bullish perpendicular call option spread positions only when the stock price move needed for maximum profit is less than 15% from the stock's price at the time of spread entry.

Keep Breakeven Point at Low Level

Enter into bullish perpendicular call option spreads only when the breakeven point at expiration is less than 10% from the stock's price at the time of spread entry.

Cash Out Early If You Can

After entering into a bullish perpendicular call option spread, be alert to opportunities to liquidate both sides of the spread before the expiration. These opportunities usually occur when a stock price move carries the stock price substantially above the strike price in the short call portion of the spread.

Avoid Any Possibility of Exercise on the Short Call Position

Once you have entered into a bullish perpendicular call option spread position, you must keep a watchful eye on the position any time the stock price rises sufficiently above the short call strike price. The short call may begin to trade with little time premium. Little time premium on a short call makes exercise a very real threat. Should you be called, you will have stock expenses to sell the stock, as well as stock commissions to buy the stock by exercising the long calls. These extra expenses incurred from an exercise would erode a lot of the profit locked in by the favorable differences in the strike prices.

CHAPTER 25

Five Questionable Strategies That Could Increase Your Blood Pressure and Your Losses

The preceding 24 chapters discussed the most familiar and widely known option strategies. This last chapter deals briefly with some of the less-well-known and less-often-used option strategies. If you classify yourself as a *conservative* investor, these strategies are not for you. They are used primarily by investors of sophistication and expertise in the arena of option trading.

THE CALL OPTION MONEY SPREAD STRATEGY

In this strategy, you sell more than one (usually two) high strike price call option backed only by the ownership of a lower strike price call option. The expiration month is the same in both options.

Objective

Your objective in establishing a call option money spread is to collect enough premium dollars from the sale of the high strike price calls to cover the entire cost of the long call(s) bought and to ensure a profit even if the underlying stock were to go to zero during the life of the options.

Risk

Your risk of loss lies only in a price rise in the underlying stock that carries the stock price above a predeterminable risk point. Above that point, your risk becomes unlimited.

Profit Potential

Your profit potential is limited to the strike price difference between the low strike price call(s) you own and the high strike price call(s) you issued, plus any premium excess of calls you sell over calls bought reduced by the cost of commissions.

Defenses against Unlimited Risk

When you execute a call option money spread, you should preplan defensive actions that you will implement should the underlying stock breach the predetermined upside risk point.

Defense I.   Buy offsetting call(s) to eliminate any uncovered call position.

Defense II.   Buy the necessary shares of underlying stock to cover any uncovered call obligations.

Example: A Call Option Money Spread

Stock XYZ is 105. In April you execute the following orders: Sell 2 July XYZ 115s at 5 for $1,000, and buy 1 July XYZ 110 at 7 for $700. In this example your precommission excess of premium received over premium paid is $300. There is no downside risk. The upside risk point is approximately $121.

THE HORIZONTAL PUT OPTION SPREAD STRATEGY

In this strategy you sell a near-month put option and simultaneously buy a more distant put option on the same stock. The strike price in each put is the same. The quantity of puts bought equals the quantity of puts sold.

Objective

Your objective in establishing a horizontal put option spread position is to have an out-of-pocket spread cost that is substantially less than the cost of the more distant put purchased.

Risk

Your risk of loss is limited to the out-of-pocket spread difference paid plus option commission expenses to enter the spread and later exit from it. Additional commission expense could occur if the near-month short put were exercised, thus forcing the incurrence of stock commission expenses to buy the stock and later sell it.

Profit Potential

In the horizontal put spread, you could possibly profit in two ways: (1) if the spread difference widened to the extent that both sides of the spread could be liquidated for more money than the out-of-pocket cost to establish the spread, or (2) if the near-month put expired unexercised and then the stock declined so that the far-month put could be sold for more than the out-of-pocket spread entry cost.

Defense

To protect against incurrence of stock commission expense, when you establish a horizontal put option spread position, you should plan to close out both sides of the spread if the near-month put sinks deep in the money to a point at which there is very little time premium above the intrinsic worth of the put.

Example: A Horizontal Put Option Spread

In early April, you decide to establish a horizontal put option spread position in XYZ, which is $40. You execute the following orders: Sell 5 May XYZ 40 puts at 2$^1/_2$ for $1,250, and buy 5 July XYZ 40 puts at 3$^1/_2$ for $1,750. In this example, your out-of-pocket spread difference is $500 plus the option commissions.

THE BULLISH PERPENDICULAR PUT OPTION SPREAD STRATEGY

You issue on the same stock an in-the-money put with a substantial time premium, and you hedge the short put position through the purchase of an out-of-the-money long put. The expiration month is the same for both puts. The in-the-money put has a higher strike price than the out-of-the-money put. The quantity of puts sold equals the quantity of puts bought.

Objective

Your objective in establishing a bullish perpendicular put option spread position is to collect a large enough premium from the high strike price put that you sell to completely cover the cost of the put you buy and to provide enough excess dollars (after all commissions) to allow for a substantial profit should your judgment that a substantial upmove in the stock price be confirmed.

Risk

Your risk of loss is limited to the difference in strike prices, less the excess premium you receive from the sale of the high strike put versus the cost of the low strike put. This risk is made greater by the option expense.

Profit Potential

Your profit potential is limited to the excess of premium received from the sale of the high strike price put versus the cost of the low strike price put, reduced by option commission expenses. The maximum profit potential at expiration is achieved if the underlying stock rises above the high strike put price and both options expire. A profit also may be earned before expiration if the underlying stock advances enough over the high strike price put to a point at which both sides could be liquidated at a net cost of less than the net proceeds received on the establishment of the spread.

Defense

To protect against an unwanted exercise that would cause you to incur commission expense, you should plan to close out both sides of the spread if the high strike price put sold goes deeper into the money and is trading with very little time premium over the intrinsic worth of the put.

Example: A Bullish Perpendicular Put Option Spread

In early April, you decide to establish a bullish perpendicular put option spread position. With XYZ at 39, you issue the following orders: Sell 5 XYZ July 40s at 4 for $2,000, and buy 5 XYZ July 35s at 1 for $500. In this example, your favorable net proceeds from puts sold versus puts bought are $1,500 less the option commission expense.

THE BEARISH PERPENDICULAR PUT
OPTION SPREAD STRATEGY

In this strategy, you believe that XYZ may experience a price decline. You establish a bearish perpendicular put option spread position through purchasing a put with a high strike price and issuing a put with a lower strike price. The expiration month is the same in both puts.

Objective

Your objective in establishing the bearish perpendicular put option spread position is to obtain an out-of-pocket spread cost that will be substantially less than the cost of the high strike price puts that you buy.

Risk

Your risk of loss is limited to the out-of-pocket spread difference paid plus option commission expenses to enter and later exit from the spread.

Additional commission expenses could be incurred if XYZ plunged below the strike price of the short puts issued and if the puts were exercised. This would force the investor to buy and later sell stock, incurring commissions on the purchase and the sale.

Profit Potential

Your profit potential in a bearish perpendicular put option spread is limited to the strike price difference less the net spread entry cost, adjusted for option commission expenses to enter and exit the spread. The maximum profit at expiration would occur if XYZ were at the low strike price, if the short XYZ low strike price puts were to expire, and if the long high strike price puts were sold for their intrinsic worth.

Defense

To protect against incurrence of stock commission expenses, you should plan to close out both sides of the spread if the low strike price put that you issued went deep in the money to where it was trading for little time premium over the intrinsic worth of the put.

Example: A Bearish Perpendicular Put Option Spread

In early April, you decide to establish a bearish perpendicular put option spread position. You execute the following orders with XYZ at 39: Buy 5

XYZ July 45 puts at 6^1/$_2$ for $3,250, and sell 5 XYZ July 40 puts at 3 for $1,500. In this example, you incur an out-of-pocket expense of $1,750 from the excess cost of puts bought over puts sold. The option commission expense increases the out-of-pocket cost.

WRITING OUT-OF-THE-MONEY NAKED COMBINATIONS

In this particular strategy, you typically issue an out-of-the-money call option and an out-of-the-money put option on the same underlying stock. The expiration month is usually the same but can be different according to your choice.

Objective

Your objective in writing naked out-of-the-money combinations is to collect two advance premiums and provide a wide zone within which the stock can fluctuate without threat of either the short call or the short put being exercised.

Risk

The risk in writing out-of-the-money naked combinations can be very great. If the underlying stock rises above the strike price in the short call obligation, the risk becomes unlimited. If the stock declines below the strike price in the short put obligation, the risk is limited only by the stock trading at zero. Both risks are mitigated only by the net option premium you receive.

Profit Potential

Your profit potential is absolutely limited to the two option premiums you receive, and it is reduced by the option commission expenses.

Defenses

If you execute out-of-the-money naked combinations, you should preplan defensive actions to take should either the high strike price option or low strike price option obligation be in danger of being breached.

Defense of the high strike price short call option obligation would involve buying a high strike price call to offset the short call obligation, most likely incurring a loss. You would also buy an offsetting low strike price put for a small fraction to relieve any possibility of a price swing down below the low strike price short put obligation.

Defense of the low strike price short put obligation would involve buying a low strike put to offset obligation on a stock price decline that penetrates the strike price in the short put. Simultaneously with the put purchase, you would buy a high strike price call at a small fraction to offset the short call obligation.

Example: An Out-of-the-Money Naked Combination

An example of writing an out-of-the money naked combination is as follows: Stock XYZ is 40. In April you execute the following orders: Sell 5 XYZ July 35 puts at 1 1/2 for $750, and sell 5 XYZ July 45 calls at 2 for $1,000.

In this example, you collect two premiums totaling $1,750 less the option commission expense. As long as XYZ remains over 35 and under 45, you will earn the entire premium less the option commission. A substantial move above the high strike or below the low strike places you at risk.

There is an end to all things, and so it is with this book. Difficult and complex as some of the option strategies are, perhaps you have gained enough understanding to know:

- Which strategies you should avoid.
- Which strategies you might be able to employ in your particular investment situation.
- How to give orders to your broker.
- How to read and understand option tables.

Just one or two of the strategies properly used by you may earn you thousands of dollars each year for the rest of your investing life!

Avoidance of certain option strategies that offer high risk and low profit potential may save you thousands of dollars as well as hours of anguish.

My best wishes to you for investment success, health, and happiness!

Glossary

Assignment. A designation that indicates that an option writer has been selected to fulfill an obligation to sell stock (call option writer) or buy stock (put option writer).

Auction market. A market in which sales result from competing bids and offers rather than from posted prices.

Averaging. The practice of buying or selling the same security at varying prices. Buying higher is averaging up. Buying lower is averaging down.

Bear stock market. A market condition in which current stock prices are substantially lower than recent, or historic, prices.

Bearish option writer. A call option writer who has no position in the stock underlying the call option or who is short the stock underlying the put. One who takes the risk of a stock price rise.

Bearish perpendicular put option spread. An option strategy involving the purchase of a high strike price put versus the sale of a low strike put for the same expiration month and on the same underlying stock.

Break even point. A level of stock price on an option strategy at which the investor would break even (including commission) upon exiting from the strategy.

Bull stock market. A market condition in which current stock prices are substantially higher than recent, or historic, prices.

Bullish perpendicular call option spread. An option strategy involving the sale of a high strike price call versus the purchase of a low strike price call for the same expiration month and on the same underlying stock.

Bullish perpendicular put option spread. An option strategy involving the sale of a high strike price put versus the purchase of a low strike price put for the same expiration month on the same underlying stock.

Calendar spread. An option strategy in which the investor issues a near-month option (put or call) hedged by a purchase of a more distant option of the same type and for the same strike price.

Call option. Initially the right of a holder to buy (or the obligation of an issuer to deliver) 100 shares of a named stock for a set time period and at a fixed price. Upon exercise, the contract may be adjusted for stock splits, stock dividends, rights, warrants, or other securities that go ex-dividend within the life of the option.

CBOE. An abbreviation for the Chicago Board Options Exchange, a leading options exchange.

Collateral. Money, bonds, stocks, mutual fund shares, or other securities pledged to a broker to secure a loan.

Cover. A word used to indicate the closing of a short position in a stock or an option through an offsetting purchase.

Debit balance. The amount owed to a brokerage firm in a margin account.

Dollar cost averaging. An investment strategy involving the periodic investment of relatively equal amounts of money in the same securities and over a period of time.

Equity. The investor's ownership interest in the account (or security). The amount that would remain if all claims against the account (or security) were satisfied.

Execution. The consummation of a transaction to buy or to sell.

Expiration date. A date specified in the option contract after which all rights of the holder expire and all obligations of the issuer cease. Currently the expiration date in all listed option contracts is the Saturday after the third Friday in the expiration month.

Full-service commission. The representative full list price of commissions charged by major brokerage firms.

Good-'til cancelled (GTC) order. An order left with a broker to buy or to sell at a stipulated price until the order is canceled or fulfilled.

Holder. One who owns an option or stock or other security.

In the money. A term used to indicate that a call option or a put option has some intrinsic value.

Initial margin. The amount of cash, or loan value of securities, that an investor is required to deposit to secure transactions made in a margin account.

Intrinsic value. The basic value in a call option where the stock price exceeds the strike price. The basic value in a put option where stock price is less than the put strike price.

Lapsed option. A put or a call that has expired unexercised.

Leg. The process of establishing one part of an anticipated strategy to consist of two or more parts.

Leverage. A use of borrowed money or securities that magnifies gain potential and also increases loss potential.

Limit order. An order to buy or to sell at a price. The order may be executed at a price more beneficial to the investor but never exceeding the limit specified.

Liquidate. A term used to denote the sale of securities into cash or the elimination of an obligation.

Long option. A put or a call option contract owned by the investor.

Margin. The amount of money or collateral deposited by a client with a brokerage firm that will allow the client to execute leveraged transactions.

Margin call. A request by the brokerage firm to the investor to deposit more funds or collateral. Failure to meet the firm's request could result in the liquidation of securities held by the brokerage firm seeking to protect its own capital.

Market order. An order given to the broker to buy or to sell the specified securities at the best price available.

Naked call option. A call option issued by a writer who does not own the underlying securities.

Naked put option. A put option issued by a writer who does not have a short position in the underlying securities.

Open interest. The number of outstanding option contracts in a particular option series that have not been the subject of closing transactions.

Opening transaction. A transaction that establishes the investor's option position in a particular option.

Option writing. The practice of issuing put and call contracts in return for premiums received the next business day.

Out of the money. A term that indicates an option (put or call) has no real intrinsic worth.

Put option. Initially the right of a holder to sell (or the obligation of an issuer to buy) 100 shares of a named stock for a set period of time and for a fixed price. Upon exercise, the contract may be adjusted for stock splits, stock dividends, rights, warrants, or other securities that go ex-dividend within the life of the option.

Ratio writing. An option strategy in which the number of shares underlying the short option issued is greater than the number of shares underlying the long options held (or in long stock owned) on the same underlying stock.

Roll down. An option writer's term for the practice of buying in a short call option and issuing a new call option at a lower strike price than the one specified in the first written call.

Roll out. An option writer's term for the practice of buying in a written call option and issuing a new call option at the same strike price but for a longer period of time.

Roll up. An option writer's term for the practice of buying in a short call option and issuing a new call option with a higher strike price than the one specified in the first written call.

Short option. A put or a call option issued by an option writer that obligates the writer to buy stock in the case of a put issuance or to sell stock in the case of a call issuance.

Spread order.   An order given to effect the purchase and the sale of option contracts simultaneously at a specified difference between the two executions.

Straddle.   The purchase or the sale of an equal quantity of puts and calls on the same underlying stock for the same expiration months and at the same strike price.

Strike price.   The price specified in the option contract at which the option may be exercised (adjusted as per terms of the contract). Also known as *exercise price.*

Striking price intervals.   The numerical distance between striking prices on the same underlying stock.

Total return.   The return an investor receives during a time period from cash dividends, option premiums, and capital gains. The return is calculated after all commissions and is based on the capital invested.

Type.   A term categorizing an option as a put type or a call type.

Uncovered option position.   A short call option position not backed by the ownership of the underlying securities or by securities freely convertible into the underlying securities. A short put option position in which the writer is not short the underlying securities.

Uptick.   A price higher than the last different price.

Whipsaw.   A sharp price move in a stock followed by a quick price reversal.

Write.   A term used in the option world that is meant to be synonymous with *issue* or *grant.*

Index

Printed in the United States
60583LVS00002B/74

9 780471 315858